Fear, Adrenaline, and Excitement

by

Jack Holder

ISBN: 978-1-62217-521-5

Dedication

To Darlene Tryon a twenty six year Air Force combat veteran, my Program Manager, a key member of my support team and most of all my dear friend.

Acknowledgments

I would like to thank the following gentlemen for all their support in promotion of this book:

Marty Baum, my friend and Real Estate Instructor
Travis Brasher, Brand Ambassador of Travis Matthew Apparel
Dennis Gardner, U.S. Navy Veteran
Rick Perry, Former Governor of Texas
Last but not least, retired Rear Admirals Jim Symonds and Denny Wisely for their support in getting approval for me to go aboard the U.S.S. Midway and present my book.

Special Acknowledgements:
1. Larry Duncan, neighbor and friend
2. Joe Reardon, my good friend
3. Don Robins, friend and golfing buddy
4. Jarom A. Stradling, my friend and Dentist
5. Mark Whitaker, friend and photographer

Jack Holder, 18 years old.   *Jack Holder, 94 years old.*

The heat of battle can best be described in three words: fear, adrenaline and excitement. Make no mistake about it, there is always a brief moment of fear. But there is a vast difference between the moment of fear and being afraid. Being afraid is long lasting and promotes bad decisions. But when the adrenaline starts to flow, the moment of fear changes to…excitement.

– Jack Holder

Contents

Prologue

Childhood grooms the man as time decides his future.

HUNKERED DOWN BEHIND A FORTRESS of sandbags on December 7, 1941, I wondered if this was the day I would die. That morning I had watched as Japanese divebombers devastated Pearl Harbor. I knew that we would no longer sit on the sidelines of the war ravaging Europe. I awoke that notorious Sunday morning a simple Texas farm boy. By nightfall, my innocence stripped away, I had become a man.

Construction crews built sandbagged machine gun pits around the perimeter of Ford Island, where I was stationed, and everyone not needed for another duty was assigned to one. Ours was near the beach where our seaplanes landed, and I was lucky enough to be with some of the guys on my aircrew.

Fear is a strange thing. The attack on Pearl, as any historian or anyone who was there will tell you, was a complete surprise. We had no idea what would happen next. In the end, the Japanese devastated the Pacific Fleet docked at Pearl and went home, but we had no idea if this was the beginning of an invasion of the country. We were on tenterhooks, jumping at every sound, hunkered down in our machine gun pits and waiting for the next blow.

My two shipmates, Scribner and O'Leary, were my companions in the gun pit. We endured three days of agonizing watch behind the walls of burlap and sand. We were scared – for ourselves, for other sailors we knew, and for America. We had little contact with the officers above us, and the information we got from them was contradictory: we had defeated the Japanese, they had retreated, they were massing for another, bigger attack. All we could do was wait, pray and hope. We took turns pointing the salvaged .50 caliber machine gun at the sky, and when we weren't doing that, we were fending off the legions of mosquitoes that swarmed us. The only respite from the tension and monotony was meal-time. For breakfast we had baloney sandwiches, and for lunch we had baloney sandwiches. At dinner, we liked to mix it up with more baloney sandwiches. It was baloney, baloney, baloney for three days – and at the time we had no idea if it was going to be three days or thirty days in that hole in the ground, but we were damn glad to have those sandwiches. To this day I'm partial to a baloney sandwich, but I like to put mustard on them, something we didn't have during the attack on Pearl.

Every time we heard a ship or a plane, we tensed up and someone would man the gun. We'd search the sky, completely quiet after the first exclamations of "Oh damn" and "Here they come again." We were listening for another attack. One plane makes that droning sound we're all familiar with. Hundreds of planes make a sound like a swarm of huge bees, a sound that fills the sky. For three days we listened for that sound, scared as hell the Japanese were going to come back and finish what they'd started.

In the end, we were recalled to our barracks. We were happy to hit the mess hall and have something other than baloney, and it was great to spend a night where thousands of mosquitoes didn't steal your sleep. When we got back to our bunks, we found all our footlockers had been busted open and our clothes were gone. We had been living in the same uniforms for three days, and our clothes stank, and we stank. But it turned out that we had had it much easier than many: our lockers had been raided so that our clothes could be used for bandages. The base hospital had run out in the first day after the attack, and some smart officer had given the order to turn our extra duds into something that would save lives. I sure would have liked to change into a clean uniform when I got back the barracks, but I was happy to learn what had been done with our things. After three days of staring at the sky from behind the machine gun for no good purpose, I felt like I had finally contributed something, even if it meant standing around in my shorts waiting for the only clothes I had to dry after washing them.

Washing my filthy uniform in a bucket the guys had salvaged from the wreckage of the base reminded me of my mother, who had spent much of every Saturday when I was a boy using a washboard and hanging out our clothes to make sure my dad and I had something clean to start the week with. She was a tough woman, tough as nails, and her hands showed it: they were red and wrinkled from the lye soap she used and from the hard work on the family farm. Growing up in the America of the '20s and '30s was like living in another country compared to the life we live now.

Those were the days long before factory farming, and most folks lived in the countryside, not in the cities. And most of them, one way or another, were involved in growing food to feed a growing nation. That's what my family did: we had a small farm in Texas, and most things we did ourselves. We grew our own food, fixed our own cars, and made our own soap. Every family I knew worked hard to put food on the table, and every small farming town was a tight-knit community that worked together to try to make sure folks made it from year to year.

But that didn't mean I loved the farming life. I went to a good school, and I memorized the names of the five oceans and the seven seas as a young boy. My dad had served in World War I, and he had been to France and seen the ocean, and I wanted the same thing. I loved the land we farmed in Texas, but I knew from when I was little that I wanted more too. So in the end, I joined the Navy, like so many American boys in that age, because there was a whole world outside of Proffitt, Texas, and I wanted to see it.

Just a Boy From Texas

I WAS BORN ON DECEMBER 13, 1921, in Gunter, Texas, located thirty-five miles outside of Dallas. My dad named me after his eldest brother, Joseph Norman Holder.

We moved from Gunter to the Proffitt Community, fifty-six miles south of Wichita Falls, when I was one year old.

Jack at one year old.

My dad was two when Grandpa Holder died. Left with five small children, in time Grandma remarried a good man, my grandpa Hudson, who had five children of his own. This always reminded me of Benjamin Franklin's advice to young men to marry a widow with plenty of children to work the family land, and when I was much older, of the TV show

The Brady Bunch. By the 1970s when that show was on, a family that big was an odd thing, strange enough for ABC to spend millions of dollars making a story about it. But when Dad was young – this would have been in the late 1800s, kind of hard to imagine now in 2015 – mixed families like this weren't uncommon. It was a hard life, and broken families often came together to make ends meet. It's common these days to suppose that folks born a hundred years ago were born tougher, but it seems to me that a hard life makes hard people. We were lucky when the war started to have a nation of hard men and women to serve, but in a hard world, that's what you get.

I'm ninety-four years old as I write this, and if at times I worry that young folks these days are too soft, or too entitled, on the other hand I feel like that's a part of what makes America great. Kids these days – most of them, at least – go to bed having had enough to eat, and most of them won't be called to war. So if young people aren't as tough as the men I served with in World War II, that's okay to me. Civilization is, I think, making things better for the next generation so they don't have to suffer the things those in my generation suffered. When I see a "millennial" or whatever they're calling younger people these days, I see progress. Sure, on some level I see kids who would rather talk than fight, but at the same time I know that what my dad did in World War I and what I did in the next war made it possible for them to live an easier life. My point of view is God save anyone who is called to serve as my friends and I were. By the end of my war, more than half of those friends were gone, and most of them before they reached their twenty-fifth birthday. I wouldn't wish that on anyone.

My family had property that was divided by Elm Creek. If you haven't been to Texas, you might suppose that the state is divided between Dallas, Austin and a windy wasteland outside those cities. But where we lived was pure heaven. Our land had access to water, plenty of trees, good hunting and fishing holes: all the things you wanted on a family farm in the early part of the 20th century. It meant we could feed ourselves and have enough left over to sell, giving us just enough cash money to buy things we couldn't make, like clothes, shoes, cars and a good woodburning stove to heat the house and make supper.

My pop was a farmer like all of the folks in our family, and a World War I veteran. He built his family a small four-room house on the other side of Elm Creek. Ever since I left home to join the Navy, every house I lived in was built by some contractor or another, but growing up, I lived in a home built by my father's hands.

A family farm today is a difficult proposition; competition from big corporate farms has been winnowing down the number of family farms in this country for fifty years. But back then it was even harder. We had no running water, no electricity, no phone, no bathroom and an outhouse in which we used the Sears and Roebuck catalogue for toilet paper. Our light came from kerosene lamps. Our cook stove burned wood. Another woodburning stove heated the house. The closest telephone was a mile away, and we were darned glad to have a telephone so close. Some people will find this hard to believe, but we didn't even have a key for the front door.

Without electricity, we of course had no refrigerator, so my father built what was called a "window cooler." He removed the kitchen window and built a box about four feet square, which was set into the place where the window had been. Each side was enclosed with a fine mesh screen that was covered by burlap cloth. The box had a trough that the bottom of the burlap sat in, and the trough was full of water. The wind would keep the water cool, and the water would wick up the burlap, keeping the window cooler cool (not cold, but cooler than the air).

The window cooler kept food cold enough not to spoil, but it didn't cool the rest of the house. You can imagine how hot my bedroom was during the summer months. I kept my window open, and though the air coming in was as hot as the bed, the fact that it was moving at least cooled me some. That was the way it was during the hottest months, and of course during winter, with no central heating, I slept with several quilts over me to keep from freezing.

My father's Model T was the same: in the summer it was terribly hot, even with the windows open, and in the winter it was like the North Pole, even with the canvas windows closed.

Farming in Newcastle

My parents were farmers, and the children of farmers. They knew nothing else.

Margaret and John E. Holder, Proffitt, Texas, 1935.

Having lived through the Depression, my parents knew they were on their own. They fed us by producing the food they put on our table. The three of us worked hard to get it there. Days started before the crack of dawn, milking cows. We also picked and chopped cotton. Then I walked to school, coming home to more farm chores, like feeding the chickens and hogs. I did homework by kerosene lamp, and no matter how hard the work on the farm was, my parents always made sure I did my homework.

Mother woke up before the rest of us long before dawn. Clad in a long dress and apron, she started preparing breakfast: bacon or ham, and scrambled eggs. Besides certain things like flour and sugar, every meal we had came from the family farm. People talk a lot these days about big-company farms and GMOs and the like. I don't know much about all that. But what I will say is that the bacon and eggs my mother served up every morning when I was a boy tasted better than anything you can find today.

My mother had to have her coffee. Each morning she drank several cups of hot, black coffee. As Dad and I ate, she started preparing the cornbread and buttermilk and red beans for the dinner meal, and she'd do it while drinking her coffee, getting ready for the long day of hard work ahead.

In the summer, Mother changed into her overalls so she could head out to the field after Dad and I finished breakfast. Our 360-acre farm consisted of half pasture and half cultivation. We grew cotton, corn, wheat and oats. In addition, we had a sizeable garden for Irish potatoes, green beans, okra, tomatoes, onions, squash, cantaloupe, watermelon and sweet potatoes.

Worker Hand Picking Cotton, September 21, 1936. Creator/Contributor: Claude C. "Pop" Laval, Fresno County Public Library.

Out in the field, we prepared the crops for picking cotton and maize. We used two different methods to pick cotton. "Pulling bowls" entailed pulling the entire pod from the cotton stalk. For the second method of picking cotton, I removed the cotton and seed from the pod while it remained on the stalk. My eight-foot long canvas bag draped over my shoulder and dragged on the ground beside me. As I separated the ball, I plunged my roughened hands into the two-foot opening and shoved in the cotton ball. When I had filled the bag, I took it to the scales, weighed it, dumped out the cotton and then filled it all over again.

The maize grew about six feet high. When I was a boy, it was a reach to harvest it. I cut the maize head from the stalk with a sharp knife and then threw it into the wagon beside me. My sweat coupled with the plant's dust created a terrible itch.

When darkness came, I headed to the barn to feed the hogs and chickens and then milk the cows. Squeezing the cows' tits could be hazardous when their cocklebur-infested tails slapped across my face. As tired as I would be, I tried remaining alert enough to avoid getting whipped by the tails, which often left cuts on my face. Sometimes when I was milking, I would squirt the milk at the calf. This did not sit too well with my mother.

Our family also raised and butchered hogs and cattle. Dad smoked and cured the meat in the smokehouse. We preserved the pork or beef by rubbing it with salt. These days when I buy bacon, sometimes I wonder who salt-cures it. Not a kid, I'll bet. Maybe a machine does it, or maybe a man, but sure as heck it isn't someone's child. That's what I mean about civilization and progress. It's no bad thing to have children contributing to feeding the family, but on the other hand, by the midpoint of the 20th century, America had grown to the point that children didn't have to do that kind of work. And that's progress. Kids ought to spend their time in school, learning the things they need to learn to succeed in this new world that, much of the time, is very strange to me. And that's a good thing. If a family doesn't need their children to work just to put food on the table, we've come a long way.

As an example of how much things have changed: Dad also had a milk separator in the smoke house. This device separates the butter fat from the pure milk. My parents sold milk and butter from our dairy cows and traded at Phillips Grocery Store in Newcastle. That was how it worked back then. I guess it was different in Dallas and New York and other places, but where we lived, you raised most of what you ate, traded for things you didn't have, and sold whatever little was left for cash to buy the things you couldn't find in your town, often out of the Sears and Roebuck catalog and sometimes the Montgomery Ward catalog.

Newcastle had a five-and-dime store, the place where most folks went to get the things they didn't make themselves. And like I've said, we also ordered from catalogs a lot, which was a kind of torture and pleasure: you knew whatever you ordered – maybe new shoes, or a winter coat – was on its way, but you never knew when it would arrive. Both of those things have mostly become extinct, though Amazon and other online stores have taken the place of the Sears and Roebuck catalog.

Grammar School, Proffitt, Texas

Not long after dawn one day in early September when I was just six, my mother had me in the tub. She scrubbed the dirt from my morning chores off my face, out from under my nails, and from behind my ears. She used one of those hog-bristle brushes that you hardly ever see any more, the kind people still used until not long ago to scrub wood floors. I hated that brush: it was stiff and it hurt like heck. And when I was feeling bold, like I was that day, I'd tell her that: "Ma, that hurts like heck!"

She knocked me on top of the head with the wooden back of the brush, though not as hard as she usually did.

She said, "Jack Holder, you watch that mouth!"

I was a polite kid, and I worked hard and did my chores without having to be asked twice. And it wasn't because I was afraid of Ma's willow switch (though I surely was). It was because even at six I knew that it was a hard life, and everyone had to pitch in. No family farm in Texas survived if the whole family didn't pull together. None of the kids I knew had to be told that. It was just a thing you knew.

Years later, when I was in the Navy, the kid on the bunk below me was reading a book of Joseph Conrad stories, and he took to reading a bit out loud before lights out each night. There was a line that always stuck with me: "I don't like work –no man does – but I like what is in the work – the chance to find yourself."

That's from *Heart of Darkness*, which is a great tale and later on got made into a film about war called *Apocalypse Now*. I always preferred the story to the movie, but I can't complain about Martin Sheen as an actor either.

So I wasn't ever shy of hard work, and even at six I think the work on the farm was beginning to help me find myself like Conrad said. And I really didn't mind the boar-bristle brush, or the early morning bath, and I didn't usually sass my mother. But it was the first day of school, and I was scared.

Of course I knew some of the kids that would be there, but not all of them, and plenty would be older than me and bigger. I had heard Mrs. Duncan, the kindergarten and grade school teacher, was a nice lady and was married to the principal, but that didn't make me feel much better. I didn't want to go to school, though I had long since given up on complaining about it. When my parents made up their minds, that was that.

So in less than an hour I was dressed up in my second-best (first-best was reserved for church on Sundays), including a pair of new-to-me shoes that my pop had shown me how to shine, something he had learned in the war (the one that was supposed to end all wars) and that, like everything he did, he prided himself on doing well. I admired those shoes when they sat in the wardrobe, but I hated wearing them. They were two sizes too big and they pinched in the front and rubbed blisters in the back.

Mother had wrapped my lunch in butcher's paper and tied it with twine, and I carried that in a clean sack that had at one time held corn-meal. I can't remember what she made. Could probably have been a ham sandwich, the meat fresh from the smokehouse, and the bread my ma's own. I can't remember that any more. But I remember for a treat Ma had included one of her pickles, and I loved her pickles. A pickle, it seems to me, is an amazing thing. I have nothing against cucumbers, but they're darn difficult to get excited about. But soak one in a barrel of brine and garlic and vinegar and you end up with something finer by far than what you started with.

I trudged up the dirt road a piece and then turned back and waved. Ma waved back, and I could see she was looking at the clouds on the horizon too. She was always terrified of tornadoes – and that's not a bad thing to be scared of – and I was used to her looking at the edges of the sky. So we were both scared that day.

I turned and kept walking, resenting the dust that began to dim the shine on my shoes and resenting too the pinching in front and rubbing in back. The schoolhouse was just a mile off, up over a slight rise in the distance, and as I walked I kept looking around, hoping to see one of my friends, thinking that to arrive with a pal had to be better than showing up alone with all eyes turning to me as I came through the door.

But there was no one, and the further I went, the slower I walked. And soon enough I found myself walking back toward the farm. My mother must have been watching me go the whole time, because when I finally got the courage to look up toward the house, she was still stood there, her hands on her hips. She didn't have a switch in her hand, and I was darn glad of that, but still I knew I was in for some trouble.

Ma didn't say a word. I took up a few safe paces away from her and dropped my lunch-bag and put my hands on my hips just like her. I knew if I didn't say something before she did I was going to start crying, and I sure as heck wasn't going to admit I was afraid, so I said the first thing that came to mind.

"Ma, can I have another pickle?"

She gave a short laugh and hugged me with one arm and smoothed my hair.

"Course you can. Come on in the kitchen."

In a few short minutes I had two pickles in my lunch-bag and we waved again and I started down the road. I felt a whole lot better, and once I knew Ma couldn't see me, I took my shoes and socks off and walked barefoot until I came up over the rise and could see the schoolhouse just ahead. I sat down and put my shoes back on, watching the local kids playing tag in the schoolyard, and when I stood up my friend Charlie Terry called my name and waved and I waved back and I thought maybe school was going to be okay after all.

For three of those grammar school years, I was a school janitor, along with a classmate of mine, Ray Bradshaw. We cleaned two rooms each. We swept the floors, cleaned the desks, and, during the winter, removed the ashes from a Hugh upright coal-burning store, then brought in coal for the next day. Every morning we arrived early to start the fire for the new day.

Lots of the kids rode horses to school, but my two friends, Aubrey McCarthy and Charlie Terry, and I walked the one mile each day. All that walking and farm work must have done me some good, because in 1934, at thirteen years of age, I was a member of the Proffitt Community track team. I ran the 100-yard dash and chinned the bar. I chinned the bar twenty times and tied with another participant. We had to wait two hours and then perform again. That time I went twenty-two times and placed first. I also won the 100-yard dash. I played softball, volleyball, and was captain of the basketball team for two years. We played basketball on a dirt court.

I learned to drive in a 1928 green Chevrolet coupe and got my driver's license at fourteen. In those days, the cost of a new truck was $400. One of my friends, Gene Creel, had an older brother named Red, and Red bought a new Ford car for $600. I remember that vividly, because no family I knew had the money to buy a new car for a young man. Kids worked, scrimped and saved to buy their own automobiles, though there was a service station owner in Newcastle who bought his son Preston a new Indian motorcycle for less than a hundred dollars. When a few years later I bought a used (very used) Harley Davidson, it cost me five dollars.

When I began high school, before I had a vehicle of my own, our transportation to Newcastle High School was a 1927 green Model A Ford truck driven by Jack Gates, with bench seats and canvas curtains. On cold days we practically froze as the canvas curtains flapped in the wind.

This was when I first began to realize I did not want to spend my life on a Texas farm. I knew enough about the rest of the country from radio shows and newspapers to know that there were other options. So far as I knew, folks in Hollywood and New York ate steak every day. Probably they, at least the well-off ones, ate lobster too, but I never even heard of lobster until I was in the Navy. And folks in those cities all had new cars, cars with radios and heaters that made driving in winter a pure joy. I loved my parents and my town, but by the time I was fourteen, I knew that a lifetime of hard toil on the family farm wasn't for me. I was too young then to take off on my own, and none of us in America had any idea what the forties would bring, but I was committed to seeing more of the world and having a better life than my parents and grandparents had. Until then, I did my schoolwork and played whatever sports were available to me.

Our football coach was Cy Perkins and he encouraged me to go out for the team. He never played pro ball, but he had been a star player at Texas Christian University at Forth Worth. In my first year of high school, Coach Cy put me on the track team with three other boys, including Preston Johnston – he of the Indian motorcycle – Vernon Walker, and Kyle Rote. Preston was the 440 finalist, but when Cy saw me run, he called me "longstride" and wished I had run that event. He wanted me to play halfback or running back on the football team, but by the time the season started, a new coach had arrived and he decided to put me on the line as a guard. At 120 pounds, I decided not to risk life and limb for the football team and I became a track star, captain of the basketball team and a softball player.

My talent in track and field landed me in the pentathlon. As a pentathlete, I ran the 100-yard dash, the 220-yard low hurdle and the 440-yard dash and competed in the shot put. My first year, I won first place in the county. The next year, I took first place in six county meets. The third year I won the Texas State Championship. I ran the 100-yard dash in ten seconds flat, and still today that is a commendable number.

I always felt the joy of physicality, and I was happy to compete in almost any sport. Today kids have lots of distractions, and I guess they're okay, but back then, you got outside and ran or hunted or fished, because that's the fun that was available. And I don't mind saying that pushing myself to be faster and stronger every day to win the titles I won prepared me for the rigors of the war that I never wanted.

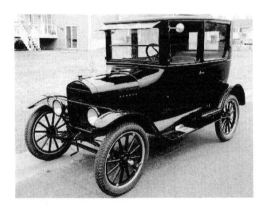

1924-Ford-Model-T.

Life these days is easy, and I don't mean that in a judgmental way; it's wonderful. I live in Arizona now, and you can get wherever you want to go without much trouble, unless you go out on the reservations where sometimes it's still only dirt roads. When I was a kid, we had one paved street: the one-lane roadway that ran between the Proffitt Community and Newcastle. Wet weather regularly rendered the more plentiful dirt roads impassable. It was an America sitting astride two ages, the modern and the past. If you lived in Dallas in the late thirties, you drove where you wanted and when you wanted, because anywhere you wanted to get to probably had paved roads. But out in the country, the small towns, it wasn't much different from America in 1850. Too much rain would turn the roads to mud, and too much snow would just trap a whole community until it melted. The war that was soon to come was an incredibly modern thing. Before motor vehicles and the network of roads that crisscrosses almost every nation now, war was a thing that you did in spring, almost like baseball. Look in any history book and you'll see that, no matter how much the French and English hated each other, a couple centuries back they only had the warm half of the calendar in which to kill each other.

Before 1800, 99% of the people in any country lived on farms, and their work was critical to feeding the people. Most roads were just dirt. So when spring came, you'd attack whoever was the bad guy that year after the planting was done and the roads were dry, but you darn sure had to win before the fall harvest and the rains came. An army in the field through winter – like George Washington at Valley Forge – could bankrupt a whole nation if all the men of age didn't have the opportunity to go home for the harvest that would see their families through the winter. It's a testament to the strength of the women and young people of America in those early days that they managed without their men and survived during the struggle for independence.

World War I changed all that. With better farming practices feeding more people, better roads and motor cars, Europe had for the first time a war that lasted the year round, for many years. My father volunteered for that one, and he paid the price later in his life.

By the time World War II rolled around – this was the war that followed the "War to End All Wars" – we had the means to fight whenever and wherever we wanted. I'm still undecided whether that's a good thing or not. When I was a boy, the seasons imposed limits and a kind of flavor on life. In winter, you spent time with family, since travel was often arduous. By spring you were ready to bust out of the house and go exploring, and in summer – as I did toward the end of my school days – you were primed for adventures far from home.

I don't miss being stuck in the house because the fall rains or winter snows made the roads impassable. I like being able to go where I want, when I want. While writing this, in October of 2015, I traveled from Arizona to Las Vegas, a trip that would have been impossible at that time of year in the thirties (and never mind that Vegas didn't even exist then). Progress, it seems to me, is a good thing. But there are things we lose with each step we take forward into the future. When I was a boy, Christmas time was a time you spent with family and close friends. And by close, I don't just mean folks you liked a whole lot; chances are they were just the folks that lived within a few miles of you. Maybe on an average day you had reservations about them, but come the holidays, they were your people, and you were darn glad to spend time with them.

I miss that part of the holidays. I like being able to fly somewhere warm to escape the cold of winter, but at the same time I miss the enforced closeness of those long-ago days, the obligation to spend time with people that maybe weren't just like you.

These days, we "put up with" people we don't like, and that's fine. It's important to be polite, because that's what civilization is. But back then, we didn't put up with people so much as accept them. Everyone was different, and you overlooked those differences. That's what America was then. We had two churches in our town, the Methodist church and the Baptist church, and folks that had been Americans since the Mayflower, and also plenty of folks that were new to America and our ways. People who were children or grandchildren of Germans or Mexicans or other kinds. The wonderful thing, to my way of thinking, is that, if they lived in your town, they were *yours*. They were community, almost family. If you were a Methodist of German stock and the next farm over was English folks that went to the Baptist church, well, you still had them over on Christmas because they were your neighbors. In the end, we were all Americans, and by 1941, when the Japanese attacked Pearl Harbor, that was what mattered most.

I always loved machines, cars and airplanes and motorcycles especially. Keep in mind that in the 1930s, the transcontinental railroad was only sixty-some years old, and the first Model T Ford was produced in 1908. When I was a boy, we had an appreciation for how much the world was changing every year, and at ninety-four, I can tell you that things keep on changing. When I read the papers, I know that things change even faster these days, but I'm of the mind that how quickly a computer becomes obsolete these days doesn't really compare to how world-shaking changes in technology were in the early part of the 20th century.

Back then, America was two countries, or maybe more than two. In the big cities you had electricity in every home, running water and flush toilets. And telephones and cars and even airlines that flew people from city to city, and country to country. The roads were paved, and you could call your family on the phone, and the idea of traveling to places far from where you grew up was a realistic goal.

The other America, like where I grew up, lived in a different world. If you were going to be late, you couldn't call someone and let them know; you either made darn sure you showed up on time, or the person expecting you would figure bad roads or bad weather had delayed you. If you showed up for an evening with friends hours late, folks just took it in stride, because there was much less certainty in that part of the country. Even if you had a car, muddy roads and the lack of road signs might keep you from making an appointment on time, and that was something that people understood if you didn't live in a big city.

Modern machines – cars and telephones and airplanes – and the things that made them possible – good roads, phone lines that were fixed after storms knocked them down, airports – tied this country together. I don't know much about literature, but I think it was the poet Walt Whitman who first wrote about America as one nation, a nation connected by a singular idea of every man being equal. Whitman was a man who saw the future of America, but it would be decades before his vision was made true by a national system of roads and telephone lines and airports and radio shows. A country, I think, is a measure of how it is connected; the more we experience the same things, the more we are truly one people.

By the time I was ready to learn to drive, and I got my license when I was fourteen, there were still plenty of places that were isolated. One of them was the Proffitt Community where I grew up. But even in a town of mostly dirt roads that were unpassable for a quarter of the year, the automobile allowed us to reach out to friends and family further than we ever had before. Prior to the time cars were something most families owned, you might see your relatives once a year, maybe twice, if they lived as much as a hundred miles away.

My father told me that when he was a youngster, someone told him that some day a vehicle would be built that could run as fast as a bird could fly. For me as a teenager, it seemed the new technologies brought the world closer than my parents could ever have imagined. When I think about my father telling me about growing up around the turn of the century and how much things had changed, it reminds me of parents today trying to explain to their kids what life was like before the Internet and smartphones. Now we can be in touch with the entire world, but when I was young, we were just learning to be in touch with our own country. It's a bit too easy at my age to complain about "kids these days" and their iPhones and Facebook, but I don't suppose I was much different. When I was young, a car or a motorcycle held the same promise, the idea that you could go out and meet the whole world.

Gas= 10 cents, Tax 6 cents. Total 16 cents.

Cars and better roads were the beginning of the real America, the possibility that you might go far from home and meet folks that were nothing like you. My dad had a 1924 Model T Ford that was a bear to start. It required a hand crank and plenty of time to warm up. He only drove it in pristine weather. Dad's Model T ran on gasoline.

Although it only cost fifteen cents a gallon, gas presented other challenges. Every time he drove it, my thin but solid dad would jack up the rear wheel, return to the front end and twist the crank. He insisted that jacking it up streamlined the starting process. I was skeptical. It seems like a lot of work to take a drive, I suppose. But the ten minutes it took to get the car going was nothing compared to how far you might go once you were on the road. It's a little like the Internet in the '90s: you might have to wait for the connection, and it was godawful slow when you connected, but once you were online, a whole world opened up for you to explore.

Sometime later, my father purchased a 1928 four-cylinder Chevrolet for the price of $200. At the early age of fourteen, I learned to drive in this car. The car was prone to broken drive shafts and broken rear axles. My mother frequently sheared an axle during her eight-mile trips to Fort Belknap to buy fruit. This did not sit well with my dad, but cars were simpler then, and when you busted an axle, you could replace it yourself or take it to the garage and have it done for less than a mortgage payment, unlike today.

My mother was a tough woman; though to be fair, all the mothers I knew back then were hard as nails. Mother washed and ironed, milked cows, fed chickens, worked in the field and managed to keep a pristine house. She was a tough cookie, but she had her fears and phobias.

I remember Mother would ring her hands in despair as she gazed out the kitchen window at threatening clouds gathering in the sky. She was deadly afraid of tornadoes. With alarm, she would turn to me and say, "Jack, tell your dad we need to get to the cellar."

Reluctantly, I would get up from my homework and walk to the barn. There was no use arguing with my mother when she spied any indication of a storm. But I knew my father's reaction before I arrived.

"Gosh, Jack," my dad would exclaim, "your mother wants to board up the house if she feels a drop of rain! I don't think it is necessary to go to the cellar." Dad would turn back toward the smokehouse and walk out of view. Every day there was more work to be done than hours in the day, and though he loved Mother, Dad was always reluctant to give up a day of work.

On one day when, like many other days, Mother had concerns about a storm, I delivered the message to my father and then trudged back to the house. I leaned into the whipping wind, pushing forward as if in slow motion. Mother had the cellar door open and waved me inside. She ushered me down into that large hole in the ground with a concrete top, floor and walls. The ceiling had two ventilators.

Mother smoothed her dress and secured her loose hair back into a bun. The ferocious whistle of the wind banged and battered the cellar door.

This time, Dad had miscalculated the seriousness of the storm. As the storm escalated, we could hear him hammering frantically on the door. Mother looked at the locked door and did not move.

His voice sounded faint and desperate as he cried, "Maggie, let me in."

Mother folded her arms. A satisfied look spread across her face. Over the howling wind, she shouted, "Jack, said you had work to do."

"Maggie, please," he pleaded.

Relenting, Mother finally let him in the cellar. He never teased her about her storm phobia again and she took every opportunity to remind him of the incident.

My mother was a kind Christian woman, but she had a very limited sense of humor. The one thing that scared her as much as storms was snakes. I once tested her patience by running a rope down the ventilator of our cellar as Mother stored peaches. Viewing her with one eye, I aimed the rope to slide down the back of her dress.

The grin spread across my face as Mother first wiggled uncomfortably, and then screeched and desperately grasped at her back, trying to wrench what she thought was a snake out of her dress. Howling, she bounded up the rickety plank steps. She ran into the desert heat, yanking the rope from inside her dress. I greeted her with hysterical laughter. My mother failed to see the humor and quelled my laughter with a willow switch.

Mother was not afraid to discipline me and had warned me not to get a whipping in school, as I would return home to a worse one. I still recall the sting of a willow tree limb cracking against my bare legs. She had a strict nature and was very religious, but she had a heart of gold and I was the focal point of her pride and nurturing. Despite all her responsibilities of keeping the house and laboring on the farm, my mother washed our clothes thoroughly.

She told me, "You may go to school with patched clothes, Jack, but they will be clean."

She boiled the clothes in a large cast-iron pot heated over a stack of the wood I chopped as one of my chores. Then she scrubbed the clothes on the washboard in the large galvanized washtub that sat outside of the house.

My mother was a strict disciplinarian, but it wasn't for no reason. Frank Heard, the sheriff from the town of Throckmorton, neighbored us to the east, and my friend Charlie Terry's family lived to the west. Charlie was as short and stout as I was lanky and skinny. We surveyed the neighborhood for fun in the limited time we had between school, chores and homework. Frank Heard adored his property and attended to it fanatically. One spring afternoon, Charlie and I stalked Frank as he vigorously dug deep holes along the perimeter of his property. Frank meticulously placed pecans into the holes and then covered them with inches of mulch. Ten times Frank repeated this process. Frank wiped the sweat from his brow, gathered the shovel and planting equipment and retreated toward the barn.

As darkness fell, Charlie and I emerged from our hiding spot and descended upon the freshly planted trees. Ten times we unearthed the buried pecans and gobbled up the delicious, sweet-fleshed nuts.

In the following weeks, I saw Frank soaking his seeds. He frequented the ten spots to review the trees' progress.

"How those trees coming, Frank?" my dad hollered from our yard.

"They aren't." Frank shook his head in disbelief. "Texas must be too dry. Guess I'll need to head to Georgia or Alabama if I want pecan trees!"

"Could be varmints," my dad replied. He had no idea how right he was.

An opposition to and a liking for alcohol was always a conflict in my family. At fourteen, I gave home brewing a try. In secret, my friend Charlie and I procured a wooden Coke barrel and brought it to the large, hay-filled barn to begin our brewing. During the stifling heat of summer, the scent of fermentation spread throughout the barn. My father, onto our secret, tried to rile me, saying, "Son, I believe someone must be making some home brew. You can smell it from a great distance."

When we finally opened our first bottle of brew, it bubbled like champagne and was very ripe. That was our only attempt at home brewing.

My mother faithfully opposed alcohol. Whenever I came home as a teenager, she wanted to ensure I had not been drinking, but she had no sense of smell (I believe that's called "anosmia" these days) and would instruct my dad to smell my breath.

He never did. He wasn't much of a drinker, but I once gave him a bottle of bourbon, which he kept in the bottom of a trunk hidden from my mother. Years later he had that same bottle of bourbon in the trunk and every so often he would take a nip from it.

My maternal grandmother equally disliked alcohol. After she lost two husbands, Grandmother moved in with my uncle Arnold. Uncle Arnold was a confirmed bachelor at this point and used to doing as he pleased. One day, Grandmother discovered his stash of home brew. In order to impress upon him the evils of alcohol, she filled the jug with salt. Later on that day, Uncle Arnold came home and wanted a drink. He filled a kitchen cup and took a sip. He reacted to the overpowering saltiness by spitting out the brew and smashing the cup. Grandmother told me that Arnold broke every cup in the kitchen trying to drink that brew. That spirited woman lived for ninety-nine years and ten months. She had a sound mind until her death.

My paternal grandmother lived with us for a spell. She doted on me, even splurging for the Charles Atlas fitness series for Christmas, a true luxury at the time. The previous Christmas my parents had given me an orange, a banana and an apple. I thought Grandmother was a wonderful addition to the household.

WWI German Gas

My dad rarely spoke of his service in World War I, but I knew that he'd battled in the trenches in France. Probably we all know men who went to war, but it's worth noting that, unlike World War II, for Americans, World War I was a volunteer effort. When they asked who wanted to go overseas and save France, my dad stuck up his hand and off he went. Of course, I did not really understand the war when I was young. I just knew it had something to do with my dad gobbling up antacids and gulping down milk to keep his stomach from hurting. I overheard lots of talk about folks coming back from France or being too yellow to go over there.

Plenty of times the ones who had been courageous enough to go were men that had troubles when they got home. We didn't think of it much back then. If a man was missing part of a leg, or had lung problems from gas attacks, that was just what some men suffered, and they didn't complain about it. Back then, a veteran who couldn't sleep at night or who drank too much had "shell shock," and after my war it was "battle fatigue." Today that's "post traumatic stress disorder," a fancy name for a complicated bunch of symptoms that affect as many as 20% of veterans in any given year (and lots of people who have never been to war). Lots of things have changed in the past hundred years, but one thing that hasn't changed much was that soldiers with PTSD don't talk about it, and in a lot of cases that makes their suffering worse.

My dad returned from World War I in 1919. His service included a year in France and Germany as an ammunition man in a machine gun squad. Dad was right there in the trenches, which meant thousands of men living in the mud and cold and waiting in dread for the next attack, which might be gas, or explosive shells, or a German rush on their position.

Though Dad rarely talked about his war, he did tell me some about it. One of the things that stuck in his mind was the weather. He used to talk about the cold and the rain, and lying in muddy trenches in France, and also about how most of what they had to eat was "bully beef," which was a kind of corned beef in tins. It was the kind of story you hear for any soldier: the misery, but also the camaraderie of the men they served with. We talk about those kinds of things more these days, and I think that's a good thing.

During World War I, the Germans used gas attacks regularly to gain a battlefield advantage. The introduction of trench warfare pitted two armies close enough to each other that they could yell across the lines. But soldiers rarely ventured into the "no man's land," as they would be shot down. In order to injure, kill or debilitate the other side and gain ground, gas was employed. Both sides used a variety of chemical weapons, including tear gas, mustard gas, chlorine and, the most deadly, phosgene.

Although gas killed only 4% of soldiers in combat, it was the most dreaded and feared weapon. When implemented, a slow-moving gas cloud would travel across to the enemy's trench and crudely and un-predictably wreak havoc. Gas impacted soldiers' lungs by asphyxiating its victims. It burned through and attacked the other internal organs as well. Men would fall to the ground clutching their throats. They would twist and gasp in despair and pain. The crudest type, mustard gas, caused internal and external blisters and burned its way through the skin. Those who did recover were at higher risk of developing cancers or other deadly and painful maladies later in life. War is hell, as has been famously written, and there's a darn good reason that gas attacks have been banned since 1928.

WWI Gas Mask 1917. Library and Archives Canada.

These torturous chemical-weapons attacks killed some soldiers and injured others. My father's exposure to German gas attacks plagued him with stomach ulcers for the remainder of his life. And he was one of the lucky ones. At some point – I don't remember how old I was – I understood my dad lived with almost constant pain. He never complained, but there were plenty of days where he worked the farm when he probably should have been laid up in bed. He was in the American Legion and was fiercely proud of his country. I hope that when he was at Legion gatherings he had a chance to talk about his experiences and his injuries; as I've gotten older, I've come to understand how important that is.

On a daily basis I watched as he ingested large quantities of milk and antacids. Sometimes the attacks were more serious. I remember the August day in 1927 when Dad left the house to plow the field. I awoke to my mother nervously glancing out the window toward the field.

"What is it, Mom?" I asked.

"Your dad should have hitched up the mules by now. I don't see him. Do you see him out there?"

I looked out at the field and Dad was nowhere to be seen. Mother rushed to the barn. To her horror, she found a pool of blood spread beside the plow and the mules gathered around my dad, who had collapsed. Enlisting the neighbor's help, my mother managed to get him into our Chevrolet. At full speed, the neighbor drove us the eighteen miles to the closest hospital in Olney, Texas. Today that's probably a half-hour drive, but back then it was much longer, and every minute it took to get to Olney tore our hearts out.

Having only the memories of a six-year-old, I can't say with any accuracy how long my dad was hospitalized. The most vivid image I can recall of that terrible time is the quiet yet confident presence of Dr. Mc-Farland. He had the largest hands I had ever seen. Dr. McFarland placed those massive hands on my shoulders, and comfort seeped through me. As young as I was, I knew that my dad could die, but those hands performed surgery on my dad and saved his life. Successful stomach or any other kind of surgery represented quite an accomplishment for medicine in 1920s.

Dr. McFarland inspired me. As I heard the sound of Dr. McFarlane's step retreating down the hallway I told my mother, "I am going to be a doctor."

"Yes, Jack," my mother replied.

"I really am."

"I know, dear," she said, and then reminded me of the recent commitment I had made to a career in train engineering after hearing a train whistle earlier that week.

Nevertheless, I never forgot Dr. McFarlane. To this day I can picture those firm, consoling hands.

1934 Chevrolet Coup.

In 1936, my father purchased a 1934 Chevrolet. At fifteen years of age, I drove this car many miles. My friend Floyd Barnes's father owned a 1934 Ford pickup. We had many races in these two vehicles. They were almost equal in top speed, which was eighty miles per hour. I also made a lot of trips I was too young for. On Saturday nights, we would go to the country dances. Of course, we could not get in, but we would stand at the windows and watch the older people, happy to be having even that small adventure. Later, it so happened this was the car that took me to Wichita Falls, Texas, to join the U.S. Navy.

Long before that, one day I stood in the school playground shooting hoops. From a distance, I could see my father's '34 Chevy kicking up dust as it hauled a large crate in the trunk. I couldn't wait to get home, knowing the crate must contain the Sears and Roebuck radio from the catalogue, my anticipation mounting as I thought about listening to Amos and Andy.

Now we have hundreds of cable channels, and YouTube, and Netflix, but back then, radio shows were the thing that mesmerized young and old alike. Folks would gather around the radio and listen enraptured to the shows, and they were another thing that brought the country together. You just knew that whether you lived in Texas, California or

New York, everyone was listening to Amos and Andy or other shows like it. For the first time, every American could have the same experience, and laugh at the same jokes. It might seem like a little thing now, but it was a significant step toward making America truly a nation, and not just a bunch of people living in the same place drawn on a map.

My introduction to movies came when I walked into a canvas tent in rural Texas to see Charlie Chaplin's silent City Lights. The noisy projector transported us from a weathered temporary tent to the busy city streets inhabited by the Tramp and his blind love interest. Sitting with my ten-cent ice cream, I thought nothing could be grander.

But my favorite diversion from the farm was the traveling medicine show. Aubrey, Charlie Terry and I never missed these performances. We would gather in town to enjoy the music, comedy, juggling, flea circuses and magic tricks that accompanied the mesmerizing sales pitches. Fellows would turn their flatbed truck into a stage and present testimonials about the "miracle pills" or snake oil or ointment they were pitching. Some remedies proclaimed cures for tuberculosis, venereal disease, cancer, smoothing wrinkles, stain removal, even digestive problems. Elaborate stunts illustrated the healing powers of the performers' wares. Now and then an outfit even brought along sword- and fire-eating performers and even more unusual folks.

People throughout history have yearned for entertainment to take them away from their daily struggles and to deliver dreams of the world outside their own towns. The thirties were an amazing time in which people had radio and motion pictures that allowed them to experience other people's stories as never before. We're used to it now; we expect it. In 2015, *The Martian* – a story about an astronaut trapped on Mars – was huge. It allowed people in uncounted countries to imagine what space travel was like, and to experience a modern version of *Robinson Crusoe*.

We take that for granted now, but when I was a young man, radio stories and motion pictures were things that changed the way you looked at the world. You knew everyone was listening to them or watching them, and you knew that in some way you were all having the same experience. It's hard to explain to younger people so used to connecting to people in distant places, but those shows made the idea of traveling from Texas to California possible, and you knew when you got there that you'd have something in common with the folks that lived there. Until the war began, nationwide entertainment did more to make people feel like Americans – like a unified nation – than anything else.

Medicine Show.

I love golfing, and my lifelong love of golf began at fourteen. I played my first round when a friend invited me to his father's club, the Graham Texas Golf Club. I borrowed the members' clubs and my obsession with golf began. Today I own numerous sets of custom clubs. I try to replicate Ben Hogan's swing as well as his fashion sense. In 1957, I traveled to Fort Worth, Texas. I planned to purchase my first set of Hogan Clubs on West Pafford Street, the location of the Hogan Club Manufacturing

Plant. Just for fun, I asked the employee in attendance if I could speak with Ben.

"Do you mean Mr. Hogan?" he asked.

"Yes," I said, smiling.

The young man asked me to wait and moments later I was standing face to face with my golf hero. Ben and I looked over his stock of clubs. Ben questioned me about certain aspects of my game before settling on a set. I cherished that set of clubs for over fifty years. I guess it's always worth it to ask for what you really want. Sometimes you get it. Having met my golf hero and having had him pick out my clubs personally sure has meant a lot to me.

Ben Hogan's Famous Swing. USGA Museum.

Eventually, my father's stomach issues progressed and he could not physically manage the farm duties. In 1936, during my sophomore year, I dropped out of school to work the farm. I had noticed a change in my father, but he was a quiet man and he never complained. But one day, after feeding the hogs and chickens and milking the cows, he sat down on the stoop next to me. He had spent a long day on the tractor and told me he was struggling with his health. I knew by then that he was often in pain, but this was the first time it was so bad that he felt forced to say it aloud. I was the only child, and in those hard times, dropping out of school to work the farm was the only reasonable alternative. Dad agreed, though reluctantly. We would lose the farm if I wasn't there to take over Dad's responsibilities. Mother suggested we might sell the farm, but none of us wanted that.

I discussed our dilemma at length with the school principal, and eventually he agreed that this was the right decision. He didn't want to see me leave school, but like everyone else in town, he understood that having a family farm more often than not meant everyone making sacrifices.

In my youth, I fortunately never had to plow a field with a team of mules like my father; Dad had purchased a tractor before I took over the farm duties. I spent many hours on this vehicle, planting and plowing cotton and corn, pulling the combine to harvest wheat, barley and oats. Neighbors not lucky enough to have their own tractor hired me to assist in their chores. They would fill up the tractor with gas at fifteen cents a gallon and pay me for my labor. I made about $2.50 per day, which was a good wage back then.

Once I was available to do most of the work on the farm, my father had an opportunity to rest and recuperate. He eventually got better and I was able to return to school. When I went back, I was more resolute than ever to avoid the life of a farmer.

After I joined the Navy, Mom and Dad sold the farm and moved to Throckmorton, Texas. Dad went to work at a shoe repair and bootmaking shop, and while that is a demanding profession, it was much less hard on him than running the farm. After a year, he moved to Albany, Texas, and opened his own bootmaking shop and became an expert at the trade. While I was in the Navy, he made me a beautiful pair of leather boots. The top portion was white, and the bottoms were black, and they were stitched with green thread. My lord, those boots were a thing of beauty. Some years ago I gave those boots to Goodwill, and now I'm very sorry I did.

Aviation

The same year of Dad's surgery, another vocation piqued my interest and became my lifelong focus: aviation. My affinity for aviation could be in part a product of the times coupled with the stress of my dad's illness. In 1927, Charles Lindbergh electrified the world with his solo west-to-east conquest of the Atlantic. The dream of flying into the wild blue yonder has dominated my thoughts since I was six and never left me.

There's a magic to airplanes. I remember when, rarely, a plane flew over town, my friends and I would crane our heads back and watch it go and identify the kind of aircraft it was if we could. Boys love nothing more than to be right, to be an authority on things, and so sometimes that led to arguments. One of us might insist it was a Boeing P-12 and another would say it was for sure a Curtiss Hawk, and unless that plane landed in front of us, the argument would go on forever. I don't think boys today are any different. Whether it's an F-18 or an Osprey or even a Cessna, they'll stop what they're doing and watch until the aircraft is out of sight. Flying is one of mankind's oldest dreams, and that doesn't seem likely to change any time soon, no matter how many commercial flights the average person takes to Miami or Peoria.

The first plane I ever remember seeing up close was a Curtiss JN-1 (the "Curtiss Jenny").

The Jenny was an open-cockpit two-seater biplane, and one landed at the Proffitt Community in 1928 and offered rides for hire. I was there when it landed with my friends L.B. and Gene Creel and their father. Their father, Harvey Creel, let both of his boys take a ride. I begged him to let me go too, but he refused. It wasn't the money; he was afraid something might go wrong and he'd have to explain it to my parents.

The pilot of the Jenny took people over Elm Creek (right over the family farm), and my friends said that Elm Creek at that height looked like nothing more than a wagon track. I was heartbroken. I wanted nothing more that day than to ride in that plane, and that disappointment no doubt was one of the things that steered me toward a career in aviation.

A genetic component to my fascination with aviation may have also come into play. My maternal uncle, Earl Murray, was a pilot, and by God, I wanted to be one too. Uncle Earl flew a biplane with an open cockpit, showcasing his skills around the air show circuit. Watching in awe, bystanders filled the fairgrounds in county after county. In the fall of 1928, he spryly hopped into the cockpit and readied himself for another amazing performance. Uncle Earl delivered. Then the crowd stared in horror when he turned the plane upside down and his seat belt failed to hold him. Uncle Earl plummeted to his death. Despite this tragedy, I still felt compelled to fly.

1920s Biplane. National Museum of the United States Air Force.

My even temper and mild-mannered character consistently clashed with my attraction to thrills and danger. But I have always had an adventurous side. My best friend, Aubrey McCarthy, had a way of tapping into my wild side. The two of us went off on a couple cross-country escapades that made my mother's hair turn white.

At sixteen, I bought a Harley Davidson motorcycle for five dollars and drove with Aubrey to Shreveport, Louisiana, after school had let out for the year. I had found the bike in a scrap heap, but it had good tires and still ran. About two hundred miles into the adventure, we had run out of money completely. In order to buy gas and get home, we picked strawberries to earn a few bucks. We spent two nights in the barn of the owner of the fields, sleeping on hay and covered with canvas. We were lucky it was warm those nights.

We purchased used oil from the service stations along the Louisiana bayous. The gas stations served mostly motorboats instead of cars, and people seemed surprised to see two young men so far from home, but all in all they thought our adventure was a fine one.

We were only sixteen, but we spent some time in bars and dance halls and saw some things sixteen-year-olds probably shouldn't. When we had extra money, we bought cans of beer and shared them. The beer was Grand Prize, a brand that, like so many things, has been lost to history by now.

During one of our stops, we worked cleaning up for the owner of a bar and slept in his shed. The owner was named George Edwards, and he treated us fairly. We worked for George just long enough to afford gas and food to get us another couple hundred miles down the road.

We were unaccustomed to sharing the shoreline with alligators, which were the most exotic animal I had ever seen, and boy could they run fast when they wanted to. Fortunately for us, they spent most of their time in the water or sunning themselves.

At one point we were treated with a trip down a river, guided by two locals whose business was catching gators. We were lucky enough to see them do it once when they snared an alligator that was over eight feet long. You wouldn't believe the fight the animal put up, but in the end he lost. We never saw what they did with him after they dropped us off, but I'll say that an eight-foot gator is a lot of meat.

I don't remember exactly how long we were gone – it was most of a month, though my mother remembered it as much longer – but I recall how tired, hungry and happy to get home we were. I junked the Harley upon arrival. It had served us well, as a simple machine often will, but that trip did it in for good.

The next year, in 1938, Aubrey and I went on an even more adventurous journey that eventually landed us in Seattle, Washington. With no money but plenty of bravado, we set out in a 1928 Model A Ford. That's a distance of over two thousand miles, and most of it was on local roads. There weren't good maps of all the roads in the country back then, so plenty of times we had to just ask for directions to the next town until we could pick up the next stretch of good road.

After making it through Texas, our first stop was in Safford, Arizona. Unlike road trips nowadays, it was common to stop, work, and when you could afford it, move on down the road. We picked cotton for several days to make enough money to continue our trip. "Enough money" meant money for gas and only the most basic food, like bread, bologna and cans of beans. We slept rough on the side of the road when the weather was good, and in the car or in the homes or barns of kind people we met when it wasn't. During our stay in Safford, Aubrey and I met another broke gentleman who had just been discharged from the Navy. His name was Bob Terrell, and he aimed to get back to his home in Seattle. Although Aubrey and I had not originally had plans to travel that far, Bob talked us into it. Bob had served one hitch (four years) in the Navy on a destroyer, though I don't remember the name of his ship any more.

The three of us gradually made our way to Washington State by panhandling, sweeping out warehouses, dumping trash and washing dishes in restaurants. Bob had a great scheme: when we stopped in a town, he'd walk down the street asking for money to buy a stamp so he could send a letter home. He made a lot of money that way, and by that method and our other jobs we were able to make the whole trip.

The whole time, Bob told stories about his tour with the Navy. He had seen a lot more than any Texas farm boy, and it gave me ideas. I knew that in the Navy a man could see the world, and I also knew they had aircraft, and I had never given up on my dream of flying.

The rest of our journey only made my dream of joining the Navy stronger: we traveled up the California coast, and I'll tell you that seeing a body of water so vast was a life-changing event for me.

Our trip lasted much of the summer that year, and though my dad never said much about it, I know that, like my first big trip to Louisiana, it worried my mother something fierce. Eventually we made it to Seattle, and seeing that city on the sea and all the many ships in the harbor made my desire to join the Navy even stronger. In later years, I came to regret the worry I had caused Mother, but I never regretted my sudden love for the vast Pacific Ocean.

The next time I left home, I was on a train to Dallas and sworn into the U.S. Navy. I had told my parents that I wanted to join the Navy and see the world, and that was true, but much of my goal was to escape the drudgery and poverty of the family farm. I never told them that, because they had worked hard all their lives to provide for me, but I knew then that it wasn't the life for me.

Joining Up

BAKING IN MY GRADUATION ROBE, I waited for my name to be called. I wore a newly purchased pair of store-bought slacks and a white button-down shirt Mother found for me in town. My small class of seventeen graduates gathered outside the Methodist church. I could feel my parents' pride as I shook the principal's hand and grasped my diploma. But in my mind, I was a thousand miles away, envisioning the sea and the movement of the ships I would soon be aboard. I knew I'd miss my family and my friends, and even the farm, but nothing could have kept me in Texas at that point. I was off to see the world.

Ever since my return from my cross-country adventure with Aubrey, our Seattle companion's tales of naval glory had filled my head. I could scarcely think of anything else. My parents knew the day had to come when I would leave, though I suppose they secretly hoped I might stay. I joined up on April 24, 1940, half a year before September 16, 1940, when the president signed the Selective Training and Service Act, which proclaimed a limited national emergency and authorized the Navy to increase its personnel strength to 145,000 men. Units newly commissioned to engage in neutrality patrol had to be manned. The war was on in Europe and the Pacific, and had been for some time, but the United States was staying out of it. We shipped goods to our allies and denied oil and steel and scrap metal to the Japanese, but the nation was mostly set against getting involved.

The act represented the first peacetime draft in American history. FDR wanted to strengthen unprepared U.S. forces in case the worst should happen, which of course it soon did. The act required men from twenty-one to thirty-six to register. Ultimately, forty-five million men registered and more than ten million were inducted between November of 1941 and October of 1946. I was lucky in a way; by the time the draft began, I had had many months of training. New recruits after the war started were thrown right into the deep end, and many of them lost their lives because a year simply isn't enough time to prepare for a war that would cover the globe and last for years.

After our graduation ceremony, Aubrey sidled up to me. His hair was slicked back and he had a mischievous grin. "Going to the river tonight?" he asked.

"I have to prepare for my trip. I wish you would come with me," I said. "Like old times."

He looked away and kicked at the ground. "I can't leave my folks."

In truth, I knew he couldn't leave Charmaine, the gas station owner's daughter. Poor Aubrey could never accept that Charmaine only had eyes for Charlie Terry. We shook hands and I left to join my folks.

On April 24, 1940, I pulled on my graduation slacks and shirt, closed up my suitcase and loaded into the car with my parents. As we pulled away, I still thought Aubrey McCarthy might come bounding out of the pasture, jump in the car and enlist with me. But he never materialized. Aubrey stayed behind and instead joined the CCC, the Civilian Conservation Corps, one of FDR's New Deal programs. The last I heard of Charlie Terry, he had joined the CCC too.

Unmarried men between seventeen and twenty-three who had no work could join the CCC. The men were given food, clothing and shelter, and a wage of about $30 a month, but they had to send at least $25 of that back to their families. All over the country, the men of the CCC did an amazing amount of important and long-lasting work. They built bridges and roads, worked on conservation projects like flood control, fought fires and, most famously, made huge improvements to our amazing state and national parks. If you've ever hiked up stone steps to a waterfall in Yosemite National Park or visited the Grand Canyon or driven through the Great Smoky Mountains, chances are you've benefitted from the fine work those men did over seventy years ago.

My parents and I drove sixty-three miles to the closest naval recruiting station in Wichita Falls, Texas. We walked into the rickety building and my mother and dad stepped forward with me. I could see Mother's hand twitch as she reluctantly signed the paperwork. My dad retreated toward the corner of the small room and watched her sign. My folks probably had serious reservations about their only child enlisting, but they stood by as I raised my right hand and was sworn in for duty. My father's grip was firm. My mother said nothing as she hugged me goodbye. As tough as she was, I suspect she couldn't say a thing for fear of crying right there at the recruiting station.

I boarded the half-empty train for Dallas later that day and left my Texas boyhood behind. I had never been on a train before, and in fact this was the first train I had ever seen up close. I went from Witchita Falls to Dallas, only about 170 miles, but it was an incredibly exciting journey nonetheless. Upon arrival at the Dallas Naval Recruiting Center, they swore me in a second time. I felt sheer excitement as I boarded the next train heading to San Diego.

Soon after the train left Dallas, I began to think about what I was doing and where I was going. I had just signed a piece of paper dictating the next six years of my life. I didn't know what was ahead of me, but I trusted that it would be more exciting than the family farm.

Soon after that, I drifted off to sleep listening to the clatter of the steel wheels on the steel track. When I woke, I spent most of my time looking out the window at the scenery. My trip to Seattle had acquainted me with some of the country, but passing through the deserts of Arizona and the mountains of California impressed on me further the vastness and differences of our country. This amazing place was America, and I was part of it, and it was part of me.

I honestly never dreamt I would be involved in World War II. No one did. Despite the increasing fighting in Europe, and the president's Selective Training and Service Act, 1940 enlistees generally didn't believe the war would extend to us. The U.S. public, media and politicians held a deeply isolationist stance in 1939 and 1940. Americans felt bitter about our involvement in the First World War and the majority of the population wished to "avoid foreign entanglements," that good advice George Washington gave the nation during his farewell address. The history books tell us the Great Depression ended in 1939, though in some places you couldn't tell. People wanted to focus on domestic issues and on making the country strong again. The New Deal was working, but it still had a long way to go. We know now that the war economy quickly put the Depression to rest, but no one then or now would choose that method of doing it. Over 400,000 Americans died in the war. That's more than the entire population of Dallas in 1940. Worldwide, over 60 million perished, which was 3% of the world's population at the time.

Despite concerns from our European allies, the United States had proclaimed its neutrality officially as the Germans marched into Poland in 1939. The Neutrality Acts had been passed by Congress in the 1930s in response to the escalating trouble in Europe and Asia. Isolationism and non-interventionism dominated American opinion following its costly involvement in World War I. U.S. citizens did not want to be tangled again in foreign conflicts. But the Neutrality Acts were poorly constructed, going so far as to interpret aggressors and victims alike as "belligerents."

President Roosevelt clearly stated in a Boston campaign speech on October 30, 1940, "I have said this before, but I shall say it again and again: your boys are not going to be sent into any foreign wars." The president repeated this sentiment throughout the campaign.

I do believe, and historians have supported the notion, that as time went on President Roosevelt wanted to join the conflict to help the British survive. But the U.S. population was so steadfastly opposed to war that President Roosevelt could not disregard public sentiment. Instead, he took measures to assist the Allied forces without actually engaging in war.

Prior to the Japanese bombing of Pearl Harbor, journalists probed many of our military leaders and government officials, asking, "Do you think Japan would ever attack the United States?"

Without exception their answer was something to the effect of, "No, they would never attempt such a foolish action."

In order to understand the experiences I was about to encounter in the Pacific as well as later on in my military career in England, one must have a grasp of the causes of World War II, the nations that played a part, and the immense geographical expanse of the war.

The Axis armies fought the Allied armies in World War II. The Axis powers included three countries: Germany, Italy and Japan. Great Britain, France, the Soviet Union and the United States, along with several smaller countries, ultimately comprised the Allied forces.

The turmoil leading to World War II began at the end of World War I in 1918. The allied forces, Great Britain, France, the United States and Italy, defeated Germany at great cost to lives and finances and great destruction of property. Subsequently, the parties signed the Treaty of Versailles, which required Germany to take full responsibility for the war and pay thirty-three billion dollars in reparations. Finding that sum impossible to repay, Germany printed more money, which only increased their problems by creating inflation. In other words, German money was all but worthless. They could not pay their debt, because the value of their currency had plummeted, and soon enough their domestic economy went into a tailspin.

German economic problems worsened along with the rest of the world's when the Great Depression of 1929 hit the United States and then spread globally. For my younger readers, the recent Great Recession is probably a fair comparison as far as the way the crisis quickly spread, but in 1929, measures to head off a worst-case scenario failed (or hadn't even been invented yet). The economic devastation could be seen anywhere you went: people without jobs or homes, families standing in bread lines, and no hope to be found for any end of it.

Germany had already been teetering on the edge of total economic collapse before the Depression, and its people were looking for a solution, any solution at all. In desperation, they turned to the Nazi Party and its leader, Adolph Hitler. Hitler promised to repair the economy, to stop paying reparations for WWI, and to rebuild German military might and national pride. He was an evil man, to be sure, but there's not a place on Earth where people turn away from a strong man with big promises when times are truly desperate.

The fascist Nazi party emphasized extreme patriotism and began strengthening their army. Although this expansion of the German armed forces violated the terms of the Treaty of Versailles, which limited how many soldiers, guns and ships Germany could have, England and France ignored it. This appeasement would lead to further overreaching by Germany.

Hitler aligned himself with Benito Mussolini of Italy and made a pact with the generals who led Japan. Each member of this group, known as the Axis Powers, began to invade resource-rich or strategically important land belonging to other countries. Japan took over China, Italy invaded Ethiopia, and Germany annexed Austria.

In 1938, British and French leaders met with Hitler. In a mistaken attempt to end further aggression, the leaders agreed that Germany could take over parts of Czechoslovakia. The British and French leaders rationalized that the Austrian and Czech lands had belonged to Germany before World War I and weren't worth fighting over.

Then, on September 1, 1939, Germany invaded Poland. This "blitzkrieg," or lightning war, began World War II. Initially, the Soviet Union was allied with Germany and split possession of Poland with the Germans. But in 1941, Germany invaded the Soviet Union, thus the Soviets joined the Allies.

The United States had not entered the war, but supplied naval support, weapons and equipment to the British. The United States tried to stop Japan with a trade embargo, an attempt to deny them the resources they needed to continue their invasion of China and other parts of Asia.

I experienced the devastation of Japan's response to the embargo when they bombed Pearl Harbor on December 7, 1941. The United States immediately declared war on Japan, and Italy and Germany declared war on the United States.

In a way, I was fortunate to participate in what is often called the "good war." Once Pearl was attacked, America's long period of isolationism came to an end, and the whole nation immediately began pulling together in order to win. It was a fine example of the line in President Kennedy's famous speech: "Ask not what your country can do for you, but what you can do for your country." That's the way people were after December of 1941, because failure might mean the end of America entirely.

We went to war to defend our nation, but in the end we had the great fortune to be in the position to help lots of other countries, particularly France, England and China. It's common anymore for politicians and other folks to score points by saying disparaging things about, for example, the French, but it seems to me the way siblings or friends bicker and argue. On the other side too, lots of impolite things are said about America. The thing to remember, if I might, is that even seventy years after the end of the war, there's still a bond. The French might not like us all the time, but don't doubt they are appreciative of the assistance we gave them. They surely are.

We can look at the changes in Germany and Japan also to understand the appropriateness of calling World War II "the good war." In just a few generations, the most feared nations on Earth have become impressive democratic nations that are important in world politics. The Greeks still have complaints about the Nazis, but despite (or because of) that, during the recent global recession, Germany took the lead in the economic bailout that kept the situation in Greece from becoming even worse. Also, after the war, Japan gave up its imperialistic intentions and has become an important player in world politics, and one focused on world peace. So, yes, I think, despite the losses and tragedies, the war I served in was a good war.

Things are a lot more complicated now. The nation and the world remain divided on the wisdom and value of the Vietnam War and the various Gulf wars. When veterans came home in my day, we were appreciated and told we had done something good. It's not like that anymore, or at least not everywhere. When the war you fought in isn't a "good war," then some will think you're not a good person, I suppose. And that's got to make coming home a lot more difficult for veterans.

Once the United States entered the war, all Americans did their part for the war effort. Henry Ford altered his assembly lines to build for the military. His assembly line was one mile long, and among other things, he built aircraft.

The B-24 had a Davis Wing, which was very narrow, and was too small for a normal-sized person to get inside and shoot and buck rivets. Henry Ford went to Galveston, Texas, and hired every little person ("midget" was the term we used back then) that worked for the Barnum & Bailey and Ringling Brothers Circus to work inside the wings. Their size gave them an advantage in assembling planes.

Henry Ford and his people produced a B-24 every hour. They built a total of eleven thousand aircraft. Think about that for a moment: if you were to walk all the way around the buildings that housed the assembly line, by the time you got back to where you started, a brand-new plane would be coming off the line.

The Allied Forces fought World War II in three theaters: the Pacific, France and North Africa. I fought battles in two of these theaters, the Pacific and France.

My naval career began a short time before the United States entered the war. At that time, the training of recruits for the Navy was carried on at four widely separated establishments, all of which had been in existence since World War I, or before. These stations were in Newport, Rhode Island; Great Lakes, Illinois; Norfolk, Virginia; and San Diego, California.

The fourth naval training station, in San Diego, was established in 1917 during World War I. Originally, the training station consisted of a group of tents in Balboa Park, which is one of the beautiful highlights of that wonderful city. In 1923, the Navy developed a permanent training station north of the city, overlooking the bay. By 1939, the station had facilities enough to provide accommodations for five thousand recruits.

During my train trip from Texas for boot camp in San Diego, I could not contain my excitement. I found a window seat and watched Texas slip away. A distinguished-looking gentleman sat across the aisle. He removed his hat and made himself comfortable.

"Son, you look chipper," he said with a smile.

"Yes sir. I am heading to San Diego." I grinned. "Just joined up."

"Well, you best get some rest. They will keep you on your toes when you arrive, I imagine."

Taking his kindly advice, I snuggled into the seat as best I could and let the rhythm of the train lull me into sleep. I awoke in the darkness nauseous with a dull pain in my navel. I twisted and turned trying to ease the pain, but soon it got worse and seemed to move lower. I tossed in any direction I thought would minimize my discomfort. Suddenly, I dashed to the train's bathroom. I vomited for what seemed like an eternity. Dazed, I fumbled out of the restroom compartment. As I moved through the shaking train, the floor appeared to roll, and I stumbled back for fear I would be sick again. Finally, I progressed to my car and staggered toward my seat. The gentleman stirred.

"Boy, are you all right? You look like the dickens."

Every movement delivered a stabbing pain as he helped settle me back into the wooden seat.

"You are burning up," he said.

"My stomach, I feel terrible," I said. "I don't know what's happening."

As the hours wore on, the pain increased and my abdomen swelled. I suffered with every movement. The man sat next to me and tried to offer comfort as we traveled the last few hours.

I waved to the man as I was carried into an ambulance and taken to the naval hospital in San Diego. I immediately underwent emergency surgery for an appendectomy.

My hospital vigil for my dad so many years before haunted me as I studied the barren walls of the military hospital, waiting to be operated on. Every daunting possibility consumed my thoughts. Would I ever realize all the experiences and dreams I had about the Navy? I wanted to serve my country and see the world. At that moment, I wondered if I'd ever even see my barracks.

I felt doomed as the orderlies wheeled me into the operating room. Modern anesthesia did not exist. The nurse gave me a mild sedative and a spinal injection to deaden the nerves. Bound to the operating table, I tried to stay as still as possible. The nurses draped a canvas shield over my upper body. It blocked my view of my lower extremities. Although I could not see the doctor plunging his instruments into my abdomen, I felt a thick pinching and random tugging in and outside of my stomach. The clatter of the metal instruments dropping into basins clanged in my ears. The tugging became a painful pull, and finally the doctor announced the appendix was out.

The nurses offered me comfort while I recovered, but a gnawing loneliness coupled with the anxiety of leaving home made for a tough initiation into the Navy. The surgery required three weeks of complete rest and recuperation. I could not do anything but lie in bed. My naval career so far was not what I had anticipated.

In Texas pastures, the prickly pear grows abundantly. Cows eat the prickly pears. My last job just prior to joining the Navy was cutting the pears with a long-handled shovel, piling pears to dry and then burning them. I had calluses on my hands like you would not believe.

The doctor examining me asked, "What in hell have you been doing, son?"

"Well, sir," I told him, "I guess I been doing what I was told, cutting prickly pears. Farm life's like that. The prickly pears can't win, but," I nodded at my hands, "they get their licks in. I joined the Navy so I could have a life of leisure." It was the best I could do as a joke, but the doctor smiled anyway.

"Son, plenty of people have died of a burst appendix, so I guess your days are going to get a lot easier from here on out. Best of luck to you."

Finally on the mend, I entered boot camp. The discipline and intimidation began the moment the company commander entered the field. Commander Sartorius addressed us sternly as we stood at attention. "I want you boys to round out those white hats," he said, referring to the new recruits' tendency to try and straighten the stiff, formal white hat issued to us upon arrival. "I know some of you are pretty salty, but most of you still smell like cowshit."

That embarrassed me some, but it also made me want to laugh (though I didn't dare). The commander was no doubt right in my case, and lots of the boys in my unit had come from farms and small towns all over the country. Most of us had never seen the ocean before arriving in San Diego. We were the least salty young men you'd ever meet, and I'd bet if you checked our shoes you might indeed smell the cowshit still on them. The Navy was going to remake us, turn us into men and salty ones at that, and we were eager and ready.

We arose at four in the morning and filed into the mess hall for breakfast, followed by hours and hours of marching. On the drill field we practiced standing at attention or parade rest, listening to the company commander's directives. The rest of the day entailed swimming classes, boxing practice and tying knots. I was thankful that my goofy twin uncles Ewell and Newell had thrown me in Elm Creek when I was three, because I knew how to swim and some of the boys in my unit didn't.

Although I did not appreciate their gruffness at the time, their version of sink-or-swim lessons was precisely the preparation I needed. The Navy relentlessly tested our swimming, lifesaving techniques, and ability to scramble down a cargo net. If nothing else, by the end of basic, we could all swim, climb, tie knots and throw a punch. It's not everything you need to know as a man, but it's a darn good start.

We received semaphore training, a method of sending messages ship to ship. It required moving flags in different positions. Each hand position signified a different letter of the alphabet. Today, you just call people from your smartphone, but when I joined the Navy, despite that we had radios, a lot of the time communication from ship to ship was one guy with binoculars watching another guy waving flags around.

After a strenuous day, we washed our clothes and hung them on a clothesline. Even this simple activity had strict rules, even stricter than my mom's. The clothes had to be tied to the clothesline with a specific knot by a short piece of white line. If the prescribed technique was not followed to the letter, the sailor paid for it on the drill field the following day. I made one mistake and learned my lesson following a day of torture on the field. By the time I hit my bunk, I was exhausted. But I never made another mistake tying knots.

Following completion of the two-month boot camp training, I applied to and was accepted for an additional four months of training in aviation machinist mate school, which was a misnomer. The training focused on aviation mechanics. We weren't making airplanes; we were fixing them. And when the war finally began, that was an important skill.

Jack's Company 32, July 24, 1940. Jack is in the 3rd row, number 7 from left side.

The Navy assigned me to Pearl Harbor. The voyage itself from San Diego to Pearl Harbor was exceptionally treacherous. I ended up on a Navy tanker, the U.S.S. Platte, barreling full speed from San Diego to Hawaii. According to the ship's company, the captain wanted to spend Christmas back in San Diego. Displeased to have to embark on the trip, he kept the vessel at full speed despite a huge storm and six million gallons of fuel oil aboard. The heaviness of the ship coupled with its speed resulted in only three feet of freeboard, the distance between the top of the deck and the water. When you went out on deck to smoke, you could almost touch the sea from the gunwale. It was like serving on a ten-million-dollar canoe.

Photo No. 80-G-12235. USS Platte (AO-24) on 24 August 1942

U.S.S. Platte. NavSource.

The sleeping quarters were in the bow of the ship. The bunks consisted of a strip of canvas stretched across a metal frame. The entire company was petrified by how low we sat in the water. When the bow of the ship came up, you were literally pinned to the bunk. When the bow dipped, you would momentarily be floating in thin air. No one slept. The ship's normal speed during such a storm should have been six or eight knots. We bashed through the huge waves at between twelve and fifteen knots.

Fortunately, the storm lasted only one of the six days we spent at sea, but it was a good introduction to the Navy. Fear, adrenaline and little sleep: that was adventure, apparently. I didn't know it when I enlisted, but it was what I had signed up for when I left Texas. I'll always look for the silver lining, and I guess in this case the experience revealed that even in violent conditions, I was not prone to seasickness. I will spare you the details about how many of my shipmates did not have this advantage.

An Assignment in Paradise

Having survived the harrowing voyage, the indescribable Pacific paradise of Hawaii lay before me. I had survived a burst appendix, and I had seen the ocean. In San Diego, one night some of my fellow sailors said, "Let's go out tonight and eat some lobster."

Well, I had never heard of lobster, much less seen one. I asked a friend what it was like, and he said, "Do you like butter?"

"Of course I like butter," I told him.

"Then you're going to love lobster."

And I did. I was having the adventure I wanted when I said goodbye to my mother and father. But nothing could have prepared me for Hawaii. The sky was blue, and the water was even more blue. Every beach was more beautiful than the last, and the local people were too.

We had fish in Texas, mostly freshwater kinds like perch and bass and catfish, but in Hawaii, the fish were so many and so new to me I couldn't remember all their names. When it rained, you expected Noah to come floating by in the Ark, but the rest of the time it was paradise. Sure, some days it was darn hot and humid, but at night the temperature was perfect, even in winter. I guess that there are things about being in the Navy I might complain about, but having a base at Pearl sure isn't one of them. One of my first nights, I asked a guy in my barracks if they had lobster in Hawaii and he just laughed.

He said, "Son, the only thing they don't got here is snow."

Upon arrival in Pearl Harbor, I went straight to the VP-23 PBY squadron based on Ford Island. I was instructed to check in with Lieutenant Commander Massie Hughes. The PBY – the Catalina Flying Boat – was an airplane that every branch of the American military used during the war. While it could be pulled onto shore and fitted with wheels for a feet-dry landing, always it landed on water. The hull was like a boat, not like the pontoon-rigged planes that are common in Alaskan backcountry flying.

The PBY wasn't a high-performance aircraft like the famous P-51 Mustang, but boy was it versatile. PBYs were used for search and rescue, for convoy escort duties, for anti-submarine patrols, as bombers, and, in a pinch, for cargo transport. The plane was so reliable that they weren't retired from the Navy and the other services until 1980, and even after that they were refitted to serve as waterbombers to fight fires. They're still flying today, in active service over eighty years since they first rolled off the assembly line. That's like using a Model A Ford as a police car in 2015. Whoever designed the PBY deserves a damn medal, that's what I think.

My new commander, U.S. Navy Rear Admiral Francis Massie Hughes, had a grand reputation. He graduated in 1923 from the United States Naval Academy. Hughes served on the battleship U.S.S. *Texas* and the cruiser U.S.S. *Chicago*. In 1931, he became a pilot at Pensacola Naval Air Station in Florida.

We didn't know war was coming, but Hughes was the perfect commander, even though we didn't know it. He had experience at sea and in the air, and he made sure we were ready for anything. And not long after I arrived in Hawaii, Hughes summoned me to his office.

Checking in with Hughes meant I had to go see the man in person. I braced myself as I approached his office. In the window I could make out a robust, round-faced man seated behind the desk dramatically relaying a story to two other officers.

As I walked in, he stood up and walked around the desk. I immediately relaxed under his generous, welcoming smile.

"At ease," he said in a Tennessee drawl. "So, Holder, I hear you had a rough arrival in San Diego."

"Yes sir," I replied.

He said, "This here boy had his appendix out the day he got off the train."

The other officers nodded in respect at that.

"Were you in a lot of pain, Holder? I hear it's as bad as giving birth." His smile widened. The officers laughed.

"Not sure about that, sir. But it was awful painful," I said.

Lieutenant Commander Hughes's twang and smile won me over instantaneously.

"Very good, Holder. Head on over to the barracks and get settled. Welcome to Pearl Harbor, son."

Lieutenant Commander Hughes's no-nonsense attitude, loyalty and fair treatment of his men captured the admiration and respect of our unit. During my time in Pearl Harbor, Hughes took a shine to me and was on the verge of recommending me for officer training. The paperwork had already been signed by five other officers and was just awaiting his signature. However, when the Japanese arrived on December 7, 1941, that opportunity got lost while the whole country was suddenly dealing with more important things.

I admired him immensely, but I rarely had contact with Lieutenant Commander Hughes. For my daily duties I reported to Chief Boatswain Mate Morris, who was in charge of the beaching crew. A PBY didn't have wheels, so they'd land in the harbor and we'd tow them up to the shore and fit them with wheels so we could bring them up on land. That was "beaching" the aircraft.

Swede Segerstrom was our lead chief. Back then, unless you were in the Navy or Army, it was rare to meet folks who came from different stock, so a guy with a name like Segerstrom was called "Swede." No doubt in Minnesota or Wisconsin or wherever he was from he was called by his Christian name, but in the Navy, most of the time you got a nickname that had something to do with your family's origins or what state you were from. I knew guys called "Chicago" and "Mick" and any number of things.

That was one of the good things about the war: in a lot of ways, it was the first time that Americans really knew one another in all their differences. Had I stayed on the farm in Texas, had the war not happened, and had we not paved the nation's roads so we could meet each other, we would never have learned to appreciate the different kinds of folks America is made of. I guess today we wouldn't call a guy Swede or "Spanish Manny" or "Mike the Mick." That would be impolite. But back then, it was both a way to josh with your friends and a sign of respect for their origins.

One of the things I love about America is how used to difference we've gotten. Long after the war I met a bunch of the Navajo "Wind Talkers," Native Americans who used their language, Dine, to send communications to military units worldwide. During all the long years of the war, neither the Germans nor the Japanese ever broke that code, because it was only Native Americans who spoke Dine. To me, that's what America is: a bunch of different kinds of people pulling together to make the world a better place.

Chief Boatswains Mate Morris treated us well, and I developed a bond with him. On a few occasions I received invitations for dinner with his family. That meant a lot to me, and I suppose he knew it. I was just a kid then (though I didn't know that until the war began), and I was far from home. I didn't have any brothers or sisters, and I loved horseplay with his kids – he had a young daughter and son. His wife was kind and happy to host a young man from nowhere in Texas, and boy could she cook.

Swede Segerstrom's more reserved, Scandinavian character made him harder to get to know. I'd guess he grew up in a family similar to mine:

hard work every day and not a lot of praise. Still, I earned his approval quickly, probably because I was used to just doing what I was told no matter how hard it was. Although he never told me I had done well, every once in a while he would peer down at me from his six-foot-three height and give a solemn but appreciative nod. That always meant a lot to me, because it reminded me of home. The man in charge is in some ways always a stand-in for your father, and when you get that nod, you go to bed that night smiling no matter how hard the day was or how tired you are.

As a young recruit, I was far from becoming a plane crewmember. I worked for four months with the beach crew as my initial assignment. Attaching the beaching gear to a PBY required seven men. The main beaching gear required three men on either side of the plane, and one tailhook person. The tractor pulled the airplane out of the water, and the men attached the gear on the way out for maneuvers and to remove it upon return.

A short time after my arrival, I became the permanent tailhook, which meant I did not have to go into the water, much to the envy of my fellow beach crew. No one enjoyed submersing themselves in water day after day. I attribute this coveted assignment to Chief Boatswain Mate Morris's feeling toward me. I was also passed up on the mess cook assignment – a hated duty – thanks to him.

Consolidated Aircraft built the Catalina Flying Boat in 1935 and the updated version, the PBY, in 1939. PB stands for "patrol bomber," and the Y indicates that Consolidated Aircraft was the manufacturer. The PBYs original purpose was as a patrol and rescue vehicle, but during the war, our primary duty was anti-submarine patrol.

The PBY had a 104-foot wingspan. It was sixty feet long and eighteen feet high. It weighed 17,464 pounds when empty and could carry another 15,000 pounds in cargo. It could fly up to 18,000 feet and its cruising speed was 130 miles per hour. At the time, it was a pretty big plane, but by the end of the war, we had the B-29 Superfortress, which had a wingspan of 141 feet and had a hugely improved payload and range. The PBY and its crews should be remembered because of how much more they did than what they were originally meant to do, and in an aircraft that did far more than what it was originally designed for.

In the first year of the war, the PBY crews did anything and everything that was needed, missions that were far beyond the original design intentions for the aircraft. After the surprise attack on Pearl, the only planes in the Pacific that had the range needed to attack Japanese bases were the PBYs and B-17 Flying Fortresses. Later in the war, better aircraft for the Pacific theater were put into service, but the PBYs still flew, and their crews bravely supported the American advance across the Pacific and continued to rescue downed airmen.

The Consolidated PBY Catalina was an American flying boat,
and later an amphibious aircraft of the 1930s and 1940s produced
by Consolidated Aircraft.

PBY squadrons operated unusually. We did not fly in formation. Generally, each PBY went out alone to spot enemy ships or submarines and bomb them when the odds were good. In the event of a bombing raid or torpedo attack – if we knew the location of our targets – we went out with more than one plane. If we were on patrol and found an enemy target, we reported its location, distance from the nearest base, direction of travel and estimated speed. If a submarine was our primary target, we made the attack without waiting for reinforcements.

Following the attack on Pearl Harbor, the PBY played a vital part in winning the war. This aircraft became an integral part of my day-to-day life and service to the Navy. From July 1942 to January 1943, I flew forty-eight anti-submarine patrol missions over Guadalcanal and the Marshall and Gilbert Islands, Savo Islands, Renault, Espirito Santo, New Hebrides and all of the Solomon Islands.

After I graduated from beach crew duty, the Navy assigned me to a plane crew as a "1st Mech," or mechanic and waist hatch gunner, for six months. In October 1940, I received a promotion to plane captain. The job entailed the duties required of an Air Force flight engineer in addition to the responsibilities for maintaining their assigned aircraft. In other words, I monitored and operated every aspect of the aircraft system, and, along with the rest of the crew, flew training missions and patrols of the outlying islands nearly every day.

Lieutenant Commander Hughes planted himself in the center of the podium for every pre-flight briefing. He waited for complete silence and informed each and every crewmember of their route and distance for the day's flight. He repeated the information received from intelligence as to the location of enemy ships and subs, as well as the weather report. Despite the routine nature of the briefings, Lieutenant Commander Hughes treated each and every one solemnly and thoroughly. We knew exactly the bomb loads, the amount of ammunition and fuel, and precisely how long we could remain airborne. It was all practice at that point in time, but it prepared us for the war to come.

Our typical training flight routes traveled to and from the islands of Johnston, Palmyra, and all around the Hawaiian Islands. We also made aerial gunnery flights and practice bombing runs. Preparations for training flights and missions entailed study of the likely enemy – primarily Japanese – aircraft and ships. During the time I was training on the PBY, I learned to love Hawaii.

Pearl Harbor Prior To 12/7/1941

In all of my years on a Texas farm, I could never imagine anything or anyplace so beautiful as what laid before me on this island of paradise. Beautiful flowers, coconut trees (which I'd never seen before), rows and rows of pineapple fields, not to mention the ocean and beautiful sandy beaches, but of course, this would not be complete without mentioning the beautiful ladies with golden skin and short skirts.

When I arrived in Pearl, we sailors spent our shore leave carousing the streets of Honolulu. I was partial to a piano joint in Diamond Head. The seasoned piano player hailed from San Francisco and we exchanged stories as he played requests.

Like any young man, I yearned for female companionship. Honolulu's Hotel Street accommodated those needs. When naval ships came in, the lines at the brothels literally stretched down the block. The men felt no shame passing their afternoons in the lines as Honolulu's citizens passed by to go about their business. It was just a reality of service. The going rate was three dollars for servicemen.

According to the Honest Courtesan, a well-known cathouse, these were the rules for the prostitutes at the time of the Pearl Harbor attack:

- *She may not visit Waikiki Beach or any other beach except Kailua Beach [across the mountains from Honolulu].*
- *She may not patronize any bars or better class cafes.*
- *She may not own property or an automobile.*
- *She may not have a steady "boyfriend" or be seen on the streets with any men.*
- *She may not marry service personnel.*
- *She may not attend dances or visit golf courses.*

- *She may not ride in the front seat of a taxicab, or with a man in the back seat.*
- *She may not wire money to the mainland without permission of the madam.*
- *She may not telephone the mainland without permission of the madam.*
- *She may not change from one house to another.*
- *She may not be out of the brothel after 10:30 at night.*

During the Second World War, the demand for prostitutes from servicemen grew so large that most of the cathouses on Hotel Street simply stopped seeing local men altogether. As the prostitutes serviced around a hundred men a day, they had to be efficient. Hotel Street developed a "bullpen" system. The cathouse matron weeded out the unsavory characters and took the three dollars from appropriate customers. Each man received a poker chip, and then waited for a room. While he undressed he could hear the girl in the next room through the makeshift "wall." When it was his turn, she came in, collected the chip, examined him for signs of venereal disease, washed him and did her work.

The Honest Courtesan, Honolulu Harlots July 5, 2011.

I frequently visited a beautiful redhead from San Francisco. These encounters cost me three dollars. Despite the rules, she snuck me to her apartment on the island on occasion.

But after the bombing, the pubs and cathouses vanished. After the attack, these young ladies acted as volunteer nurses tending to the wounded. Soon afterward, they shipped back to San Francisco on the December 20 evacuation transport on the *Lurline*. Pearl Harbor's jovial atmosphere disappeared. All inhabitants maintained continued vigilance from that day to the end of the war.

Observation of Destruction

Just prior to December 7, a British heavy cruiser docked in Pearl Harbor and tied to a mooring on Ford Island. It had just escaped from a battle in the southwest Pacific. We weren't at war then, but this was my first taste of how awful it truly was.

I boarded the freshly devastated ship and walked amid bulkheads saturated in blood and fresh human remains. Many wounded sailors in agony filled the compartments. Body parts lay scattered all over the ship's decks. The stench was unbearable. It was my first exposure to the smell of blood and death. Apparently the ship had only one doctor and no nurses. Many of the crew wore slings on their arms and had patches covering their faces and eyes. Some sailors stumbled around on makeshift crutches. The captain had shrapnel wounds on his upper body, chest and shoulders.

The ship stayed only long enough to refuel and load supplies and food. I watched as it sailed away. I am not sure if the ship stayed afloat and made it back to England.

Meanwhile, the political climate between Japan and the United States became increasingly tense. In response to Japanese advances in French Indochina (which was parts of modern-day Vietnam, Laos and

Cambodia) and China, the United States, England and the Netherlands cut off all oil supplies to Japan. These countries had provided 90% of Japan's oil. The oil embargo threatened to grind the Japanese military machine to a halt.

Japan had always known its refusal to leave China would ultimately result in war with the United States. Without a source of oil to continue their advances, their only hope was to threaten the embargo countries enough to keep them out of the war and to restore the oil trade. The Japanese were determined to strike first; they knew they couldn't invade the United States, but they believed the martial vigor of their people surpassed ours and they could at least make us back down. Boy, were they wrong.

Admiral Isoroku Yamamoto, the supreme Japanese Naval Commander, decided it was imperative to knock out the main American fleet immediately. He and his staff had been planning an attack on Pearl Harbor for months, and finally it was decided to put the plan in motion. The Pacific is a big ocean, and this was before satellites or even radar, so Yamamoto's fleet was able to approach within two hundred miles of Hawaii without being detected.

A Day That Will Live in Infamy

ON SATURDAY, DECEMBER 6, 1941, I had no military requirements or flying scheduled. I relaxed, played racquetball and enjoyed an afternoon nap. I dined on pork chops, green beans and a nice green salad. For dessert I strolled over to the canteen for my ice cream, a treat I continue to enjoy. Like everyone else on that day, I was oblivious that the next day my life and the lives of all Americans would change forever.

My routine in Pearl Harbor dictated that every fourth day I had "duty," which mandated staying on board. I woke up at 0500 and completed my daily stretching exercises. After showering and shaving, I dined on the Navy's "shipwrecked ham and eggs" and a large orange juice. It was just an ordinary morning, but the day was one so extraordinary that I still remember what I had for breakfast seventy-four years later.

At 7:55 am on December 7, 1941, my section had just fallen in for muster in our hangar. I had duty, but other members of my squadron planned on heading to church, Waikiki beach, or their chosen Sunday recreational activity. As our section leader began calling roll, we heard a screaming aircraft, then a terrible explosion. We ran outside.

The neighboring VP-21 hangar just a hundred yards away had been hit by the first bomb dropped on Ford Island. It was engulfed in smoke and flames. Squadron VP-21's hangar was severely damaged. Luckily, the hangar was empty; the squadron was in the Philippines on advanced base training. My hangar did not receive a bomb, but it was riddled by machine gun fire.

Overhead, we saw several planes with the rising-sun insignia. We immediately realized what was happening. Someone in our section knew that there was a sewer line being constructed behind the hangar.

He yelled, "Let's go to the ditch."

About twenty of us followed him and jumped in the ditch. As we ran, I looked up and saw a Japanese plane circle and head straight for us. The pilot saw us, and as he approached, I helplessly clung to the side of the ditch, sure this was the end of us all. I could see the expression on his face – wide-eyed, with an expansive, toothy grin. I froze. The war had started, and I just knew I was going to die.

I'm an old man now, and it's easier for me to remember things from years ago than it is to remember things that happened six months back. But as long as I live, I'll never forget that moment: the face of the pilot, the roar of the plane's engine, and the sight of its guns aimed right at me.

The plane spat tongues of machine gun fire. Bullets landed all around me. The machine gun fire hit the dirt piled up beside the ditch, missing us by a mere three feet. Whoever it was that suggested we shelter in the ditch, that sailor saved us all that morning.

I do not know how long we clustered in the ditch. We waited until the first wave of the attack was over. I remember my hands clenching my shipmate's shoulders. Thoughts raced through my head.

God, don't let me die in this ditch.

Aside from the occasional murmur, we didn't speak. Our fear was intense, but our determination was unrelenting. If I was destined to die in this ditch, I would go down fighting. The Japanese were attacking our country, and nothing else mattered but defending it. First the fear, then the adrenaline, and then you act.

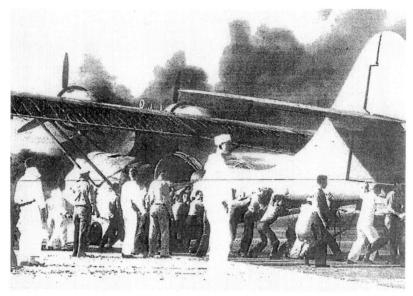

PBY Hangars. Sailors working to save planes.

When I left the ditch, I saw the devastation of the PBY hangars VP-23 and VP-21, and all of our aircraft engulfed in smoke and flames.

It was the most devastating sight I have ever seen and something I will never forget.

I knew I was in the middle of the beginning of something that would change the world and my life, and the fear that engulfed me was real. The fear soon turned to adrenaline, of wanting to know what to do, and the excitement of action came over me and turned to "What can we do to fight back?"

I immediately caught sight of our squadron captain, Captain Hughes, still wearing his red pajamas, running down the road waiving his .45 caliber and shouting, "Shoot those sons-of-bitches!"

That there is a prime example of Navy pride and good training: an officer in his PJs threatening planes armed with machine guns with a pistol accurate out to no more than a hundred feet. This country's been in enough wars, but the attack on Pearl was a different thing. It was an outrage that made men into heroes willing to do anything to defend their homeland, even something as foolish as firing a handgun at a plane going two hundred miles an hour.

But none of us saw how foolish Captain Hughes's act of defiance was that day. We were wholly convinced, caught up in it, and if we had to fight the enemy with sticks and stones, well, that's what we were going to do.

Ford Island. Sailors watch U.S.S. Shaw explode.

While the VP-21 hangar was engulfed in flames, I was directed to the VP-23 hangar by the leading chief to ready the squadron commander's plane for flight. The engines were buttoned up, the plane rolled out, refueled, and loaded with two one-thousand pound bombs. The captain and his crew flew nineteen hours searching for the Japanese task force and found nothing. That lone plane searching for a fleet at sea was just like Captain Hughes in his pajamas: there was no hope to do much good, but the act of defiance mattered more than any damage they might do.

Only two weeks prior my unit had flown these planes in from San Diego. Without them, we would have been left with nothing to fly after the hangar bombings. That was not the only lucky happenstance for the

United States. The Japanese had launched their surprise attack against the U.S. forces on a Sunday in hopes of catching the entire fleet in port.

But the aircraft carriers – which would become the bedrock of the Pacific war strategy – and one of the battleships were not in port. The U.S.S. *Enterprise* was returning from Wake Island; the U.S.S. *Lexington* was shipping aircraft to Midway; the U.S.S. *Saratoga* and U.S.S. *Colorado* were being repaired on the mainland. Admiral Nagumo, the Japanese flight admiral, ignored Japanese intelligence reports that the carriers were absent and went forward with the attack anyway. I don't doubt that we would have beaten the Japanese one way or the other, but I do think that it would have taken months or even years longer had we lost the aircraft carriers at Pearl that day.

Seventy-five minutes had elapsed between the first and second waves. Our first task was to separate the damaged from the undamaged aircraft. We had to defend the islands, and the only way to do it was to put men in the air.

The Japanese continued the attack with their force of six carriers and 423 aircraft. They launched the first wave of a two-wave attack from approximately two hundred miles north of Oahu. The first wave consisted of 183 fighters, divebombers and torpedo bombers. They struck the fleet in Pearl Harbor, Ford Island, Hickam Field, Kaneohe and EWA. Next, 167 Japanese aircraft attacked the same targets during the second wave.

When the second wave was over, I took a long look at the devastation. The destroyer *Shaw* had been hit by bombs and torpedoed in a floating dry dock across the bay from our hangar. The *Arizona, West Virginia, Tennessee, Nevada, California, Maryland* and *Oklahoma*, one behind the other, had all been hit by bombs and torpedoes. The *Arizona* was engulfed in smoke and flames, listing heavily and sinking. As most Americans know, to this day one thousand sailors remain entombed in the *Arizona*.

The Japanese torpedoed and sank the *Oklahoma*. It turned turtle up and 429 sailors perished. Four hundred and four were trapped and are entombed in the ship. Although the *Arizona* and *Oklahoma* were a total loss, the other ships were raised, repaired and returned to duty. Sailors tend to be superstitious types, and if you ask anyone who was there, they'd probably tell you that when those ships were refitted, they were pissed off and ready to take the fight to the Japanese home islands.

The *Pennsylvania* was docked abreast the naval shipyard. The *Utah* was on the opposite side of Ford Island. Badly damaged, the *Nevada* still tried to get under way. It managed to make it to the other side of Ford Island, but it was sinking, so in order to not block the harbor, it was purposely run aground. Like the *California* and others, it was later repaired.

The flames and wreckage surrounded and suffocated me with grief, but I had little time to review the damage. The raid continued for a five-hour period as six carriers sent two waves of 350 divebombers, torpedo planes and fighters. U.S. damages escalated to eight battleships, ten smaller warships, and 230 aircraft. 2,400 American soldiers and sailors were killed. Having completely taken the U.S. by surprise, Japan suffered comparatively miniscule losses. American forces shot down a mere twenty-nine planes.

It's worth taking the time – especially so many decades later – to look at the death toll and the Japanese strategy. In the end, tragically, 2,400 American servicemen were killed, nearly twenty ships sunk, and hundreds of planes destroyed during the Pearl Harbor attack. But it's important to understand that in 1941, the United States had a population of 133 million people, and it was one of the most industrialized nations in the world. Japan had a population of around 73 million, and it was far behind the U.S. in terms of industrial production.

What that means is that the Japanese strategy was based on the idea that a sudden attack would make America too fearful to join the war. This represents a complete and foolish understanding of what America and Americans are. America, by and large, is a Christian nation. But it's not a "turn the other cheek" nation. As awful as it was, the attack on Pearl did nothing more than guarantee that Japan would lose its war. When Pearl Harbor occurred, about half a million Americans served in the various branches of the military. The 2,400 killed represented around half of a percent of Americans wearing the uniform.

The attack was primarily a psychological move; it meant little in terms of how many men we could put in the field. And worse, for the Japanese: by late 1941 there were 1.8 million men in uniform, and in 1942 it was 3.9 million, and in 1943 it was nearly ten million. And we know how that story ended for Imperial Japan.

The Japanese bloodied our nose, and by the end of the war, we put them in the hospital on a ventilator. America, as others have learned to their woe, can shrug off an injury and come back stronger every time. There's an expression about how dangerous a cornered rat is. I served on Navy ships with rats, and I can tell you that's no lie. When America is attacked, we become the cornered rat, something the Japanese discovered before too long. At least some Japanese understood this. Following the raid on Pearl Harbor, Yamamoto was congratulated on his success.

He reputedly said, "I have traveled the United States; they are a very industrious nation and I am afraid we have awakened a sleeping giant."

After the attack, measures to defend our homeland went immediately into place. Troops took positions around the entire perimeter of the main Hawaiian Islands. General Walter C. Short declared martial law effective immediately. Additionally, he announced that he was taking over the Hawaiian territorial government. Blackouts, curfews, censorship and any other restriction deemed necessary by the Army came into place. The

Army took over the airports. All private planes were grounded. Troops placed barricades at shore in order to thwart a possible Japanese landing.

Photo # 80-G-32492   Machine gun emplacement at NAS Ford Island, soon after the Pearl Harbor raid

Active Machine Gun Pits at Ford Island.

By early evening, sandbag machine gun pits had been constructed all around Ford Island. The pits each housed three men. Along with my two shipmates, I occupied one of them for three days and nights. We watched and waited, never sure when and if a third wave of Japanese might materialize from the sea or sky. The complete surprise had exposed our vulnerability. Now all we could do was alternate sleeping, eating boloney sandwiches and standing watch and fighting mosquitoes.

There would be no third wave. Despite Commander Minoru Genda's – the chief planner of the raid – strong urging to send Japanese planes to strike the shore facilities, oil storage tanks and submarines, and to hunt down the American carriers they believed to be nearby, Commander Nagumo decided not to risk further action.

Of course, hunkered down in the machine gun pit, we had no way of knowing they were not returning. In our minds, every aircraft or ship noise sounded like the Japanese returning. Enveloped in darkness, unable to know what was happening outside the walls of sand, every plane engine evoked a surge of alertness and fear. After seventy-two hours, the pit reeked of our sweat and anxiety.

While I stood watch in the pit, other sailors left Pearl Harbor to pursue the Japanese. Most of the cruisers and destroyers took a southern course. The Japanese had retreated to the north, so no contact was made.

Approximately two dozen naval fighter pilots took off from the U.S.S. *Enterprise* in pursuit of the Japanese attack fleet. Six of the fighters were sent to Oahu and were subjected to friendly fire from panicked American ground troops. Three of the six pilots were shot down and killed. Two landed on Ford Island, and the final plane ran out of fuel, causing the pilot to parachute down near Barbers' Point.

Ensign Ruark and his crew flew to Palmyra, about seven hundred miles southwest of Pearl Harbor. He was part of our PBY squadron. Upon return, trying to land in Pearl Harbor in total darkness, the plane crashed into the water. U.S. naval personnel found the plane the next day. All the crew died still strapped into their seats.

For the Japanese, reaching Pearl Harbor for the initial strike had been no small feat. First they had had to learn how to refuel at sea (a technique the U.S. Navy had already worked out). To sink all those ships, they used their superb electric torpedoes and perfected shallow-water bombing tactics. The Japanese had good equipment, talented pilots, total ambush and an ingenious plan. While everyone suspected the U.S. would be dragged into the war eventually, none of us stationed in Pearl Harbor expected an attack.

Despite later rumors, there was no advance knowledge of the Japanese plan. The commanders had been complacent about routine defensive measures. Even if the defense had been more alert, the surprise and overwhelming power of the Japanese strike probably would have been decisive. Remember that this was long before the days of radar and satellite surveillance. The only way to spot an enemy was with binoculars from the deck of a ship, or from an aircraft. That means that an enemy just a few hundred miles away – the distance the Japanese launched their attack from – was functionally invisible unless you got very lucky.

On the fourth day, we returned to the barracks and found all our lockers broken into to retrieve white clothing to be used for bandages. We had been looking forward to changing into clean clothes, but we were happy to launder our filthy uniforms because we knew our clothes had gone to the hospitals where the wounded were lined up in the hallways awaiting treatment.

The Navy issued a postcard to all personnel to send home with one of two messages: "*I am wounded*" or "*I am OK*." We could say nothing more.

During my remaining time on Pearl Harbor, I heard many accounts of what other sailors experienced on that fateful morning.

As most of the first raid was on the hangars and barracks, guys in those places lay helplessly behind or under flimsy shelters while bomb splinters or machine gun bullets and debris flew around like a deadly rain.

Like me, others spent a hell of a night in a machine gun pit, watching, sleeping and fighting mosquitoes. Cold and wet from the afternoon rain, they watched the skies and stewed, discussing rumors of Japanese raiding parties.

On some ships, men reported rushing for the guns on board only to find they didn't have their firing pins installed. The men had to put them in. Then they discovered that the ammunition ready lockers and magazines were locked and the keys could not be found. They had to cut off the locks with bolt cutters. When they could finally fire, they couldn't secure hits. Frustrated and desperate, they watched the torpedoed and bombed battleships enveloped in smoke and plumes of water.

Fourteen months later, I returned home for a short leave. I knocked on the door and shouted, "A sailor out here wants to see you."

Gruffly, my dad shouted back, "You better get in this house!"

With tears in her eyes, my mother handed me the "*I'm OK.*" postcard. My parents had received the postcard on December 17, 1941, nine days after they became aware of the bombing via radio reports. My dad tried to calm my hysterical mother. But for those seemingly endless days of not knowing, Mother cried inconsolably and stayed on her knees promising God that if he spared her son's life she would devote the rest of hers to the church. My mother kept that vow and converted from the Methodist Church to the Church of Christ. She served the church unfailingly from the receipt of that postcard until her death.

My visit home was all too brief, but it was a good respite, because the war was in full swing and soon I had to go back.

Pearl Harbor came as a surprise to the U.S. forces, but the Japanese had planned the assault for twelve years. The preparations for a raid on Pearl Harbor included two years practicing on a miniature replica of Pearl Harbor. Every Japanese pilot knew exactly what their target was and where it would be.

Prior to the bombing of Pearl Harbor, the Navy had enlisted men who were aircraft pilots: AP-3C (Aircraft Pilot Third Class), AP-2C, AP-1C or Chief AP. Following December 7, all enlisted pilots were immediately advanced to officer status. Typically, an AP-3C became an ensign. An AP-2C became an ensign or a lieutenant junior grade (Lt. J.G.). Our leading chief, Swede Segerstrom, advanced to lieutenant commander, and Lieutenant Commander Hughes was advanced to captain.

The promotions were particularly appropriate, as Swede had acted as the chief fighter pilot for a squadron of enlisted men that had become so proficient they far outclassed the officer squadrons.

Aftermath

After the Pearl Harbor attack, President Roosevelt called his military staff together and directed them to devise a plan to bomb Tokyo. The advisors proclaimed the idea was impossible, as American forces did not have aircraft with that capability. It was simply too far. Roosevelt struggled to his feet and said, "Do not tell me it's impossible." And with the close of that meeting began one of the greatest tales of American military courage.

They called for Lieutenant Colonel Jimmie Doolittle, who would later become General Doolittle. His orders included selecting a group of capable pilots to begin training on short field takeoffs and landings in the B-25 Mitchell Bomber. Doolittle gathered his pilots and informed them he could not tell them the purpose of their mission, but he told them they might not return. He told them to step forward if they still wanted to participate. Without exception, the pilots stepped forward.

The B-25s were stripped of armor, and extra fuel tanks were installed. After extensive training, on April 2, 1942, only four months after the surprise attack on Pearl, the group moved onto the U.S.S. *Hornet*, an aircraft carrier, and were told their mission was to bomb Tokyo. In addition, Doolittle instructed the pilots that their aircraft had to be airborne in 457 feet (457 feet was the flight deck length of the aircraft carriers they had then). If they took 458, they would be dead. To put that in perspective, a stock B-25 with its armor intact and fully loaded with fuel and munitions generally needed over 1,000 feet of runway to get into the air. Doolittle was asking a lot of his men and his machines, and they gave him everything they had.

The plan hit a snag when, on April 18, 1942, picket boats spotted the U.S. naval task force 650 miles from Japan. Knowing their position had been reported, Admiral Bull Halsey turned the *Enterprise* and *Hor-*

net into the wind and at flank speed. The ships launched sixteen B-25 bombers. Their plan to reach their targets and then fly another 1,100 miles to destinations in China fell short by 250 miles as a result of the early launch. Seventy-four of the eighty raiders survived. One crewman was killed during bail out, two died in crashes, eight were captured after landing in China, and three of those were executed.

The Doolittle Raid attacked Tokyo and other targets. It was the first air raid to strike the Japanese Home Islands. Each bomber carried four five-hundred-pound bombs, and they dropped them on ten military and industrial targets, most of them around Tokyo. The raid let the Japanese know that we could hit them back, and news of its success, despite the losses suffered, gave Americans a needed shot in the arm. We had been hit at home, and hit hard, but Doolittle showed us and the Japanese that we weren't down for the count, not by a long shot.

Photo # NH 53420 B-25Bs take off from USS Hornet to attack Japan. 18 April 1942

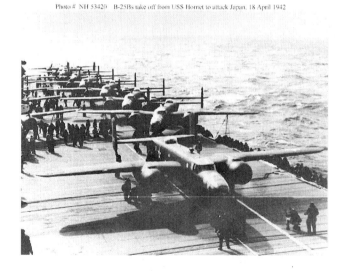

USAAF B-25B bomber lines up for takeoff from U.S.S. Hornet (CV-8) on the morning of 18 April, 1942. Official U.S. Navy Photograph, from the collections of the Naval Historical Center.

Midway

THE JAPANESE PLANNED THE ATTACK on Midway Island in retaliation for the April 18 bombing of Tokyo. Admiral Yamamoto's Japanese navy had suffered a major embarrassment from the mid-April raid on Japan's Home Islands and at the Battle of Coral Sea in early May. Yamamoto wanted to catch and destroy the U.S. Pacific Fleet's aircraft carrier strike forces. Fortunately for the United States, strong leadership foiled his plan.

Admiral Chester Nimitz (1885-1966). Official U.S. Navy Photograph, from the collections of the Naval Historical Center.

My admiration for Admiral Nimitz began while I served under his command during the war and has extended through my life. A mild-mannered Texan like me, Nimitz was the commander in chief of the Pacific Fleet from 1941 through the end of the war. The Allied forces' Pacific victory stemmed from the combined wisdom and leadership of Admiral Nimitz and from the efforts of the more colorful and notorious Douglas MacArthur.

Born in Texas in 1885, Chester W. Nimitz served in World War I as chief of staff to the commander of the U.S. Atlantic submarine force. In 1939, he became chief of the Bureau of Navigation of the U.S. Navy. After the Japanese attack on Pearl Harbor, Nimitz rose to Commander in Chief of the Pacific Fleet. In 1944, he was promoted to fleet admiral.

Despite the fact that Nimitz was not a senior admiral, FDR, when he was assistant secretary of the Navy and had opportunity to observe Nimitz, knew firsthand Nimitz's skill and intelligence.

The Allied victory in the Pacific resulted from the leadership of two very different men. The boisterous, showboating MacArthur led through intimidation, while Nimitz approached leadership in a relaxed manner. Nimitz emphasized the importance of collaboration and cooperation.

According to historian Ronald Spector, it's hard to imagine two people more different: "While MacArthur was a forceful and colorful personality, a man of dramatic gestures and rhetoric, Nimitz was soft-spoken and relaxed, a team player, a leader by example rather than exhortation."

Chester Nimitz had an unlikely path to success in the naval ranks. Although his granddad had served in the Navy, Nimitz had initially sought an appointment to West Point. Discovering the appointments had been taken, he reluctantly applied to the Naval Academy. Nimitz did well initially, but nearly tanked his career when he beached a ship under his command. Somehow, his career survived that snafu.

Nimitz's first tour was an assignment to the battleship *Ohio*. The tour predominantly focused on Japan and the Orient. Nimitz even had an introduction to Admiral Togo while in Japan. Admiral Togo would construct the Japanese navy that would become Nimitz's foe.

Nimitz became an expert in the emerging area of submarine warfare. He instructed naval cadets about the subject in 1912. During World War I, he served in the Atlantic sub force. Later, he was instrumental in the building of the submarine base at Pearl Harbor.

His most practical knowledge and expertise derived from the advanced courses he took at the Naval War College in 1922. Their exercises consistently pitted them against the Japanese. Nimitz stated that after completing those courses, nothing that happened in the Pacific at the start of World War II was strange or unexpected. Citing Nimitz's invaluable knowledge of the Japanese region, Secretary Frank Knox gave Nimitz command of the Pacific Fleet only days after the Pearl Harbor travesty.

As considerable as his tactical skills were, perhaps Nimitz's greatest gift was his leadership ability. Naval historian Robert Love writes that Nimitz possessed "a sense of inner balance and calm that steadied those around him." He also "had the ability to pick able subordinates and the courage to let them do their jobs without interference. He molded such disparate personalities as the quiet, introspective Raymond A. Spruance and the ebullient, aggressive William F. Halsey, Jr. into an effective team."

Of course, these same qualities helped ease Nimitz's relationship with MacArthur, no small feat given the amount of coordination called for between their two services. And it is fortunate that Nimitz did not share MacArthur's need for publicity; even the vast Pacific would not have been big enough for two great military leaders. Journalist Robert Sherrod, who spent time in both of their headquarters, said that "the Admiral was frequently the despair of his public relations men; it simply was not in him to make sweeping statements or to give out colorful interviews."

Midway: The War's Pivotal Battle

Aerial view of Midway.

Admiral Nimitz knew there would be retaliation after Doolittle's raid. He just didn't know where. In anticipation of a retaliatory mission, Admiral Nimitz placed intelligence forces on high alert. Intelligence honed in on coded messages containing two letter abbreviations, "AF" and "AO." The rest of the code had been broken. Intelligence had narrowed these designations to signify either Midway or the Aleutian Islands and the location of the next Japanese target. Strategically, the Japanese wanted to create military footholds on the islands standing between the United States and their homeland. Both Midway and the Aleutians fit the bill.

In order to reveal the meaning of these two-letter codes, our chief of intelligence had devised a plan to send an un-coded message regarding a fresh water condenser failure on Midway. Admiral Nimitz said to send it. The Japanese took the bait and sent their own message relaying to their forces that "AF" had a fresh water condenser failure.

Admiral Nimitz sent a small task force to the Aleutians as a diversion. The Japanese fell for that ruse too, and Japanese Fleet Admiral Yamamoto advised his forces that the U.S. Navy was headed for the Aleutians and they should move to take Midway.

Nimitz then sent the main task force to Midway, positioning the aircraft carriers in one location and the ships in another.

VP-23, my squadron, left for Midway on May 26 and began to search for the Japanese forces in the week before the battle. We had two full squadrons of PBYs and a few crews from other squadrons. We flew out of Midway on a deviated course heading of seven degrees for a distance of six hundred miles. Each plane then turned right ninety degrees for five minutes and then set a course for the return to Midway.

On June 3, 1942, we found them. Lieutenant Howard Ady and his crew from VP-23 was the first plane to sight the fleet. My aircraft, piloted by Lieutenant Junior Grade Murphy, was the second aircraft to see this armada. It looked like black pepper on a fried egg. Four aircraft carriers, battleships, cruisers, destroyers, submarines, freighters and troop ships. We imagined that this is what the fleet that attacked Pearl must have looked like from the air, and we were ready for some revenge. Their position was reported to Midway control, and we returned to Midway.

On June 4, 1942, my aircraft was airborne, carrying four five-hundred-pound bombs. At 0545, a PBY reported many planes 150 miles away headed toward Midway. Only moments later, my aircraft sighted two aircraft carriers still under a weather front at a distance of 180 miles headed toward Midway. Both sightings were radioed to Midway control.

Photo # 80-G-17056   Oil tanks burning at Midway after Japanese attack, 4 June 1942

Burning oil tank on Sand Island, June 4, 1942.

The term Midway Island is actually misnomer. It should be Midway Atoll. It is actually two small islands (each three miles across, separated by a small lagoon), Sand Island and Eastern. Much of the American presence on the island was in underground sand bunkers. We ate and slept in these underground bunkers.

On June 4 at 0645, Japanese forces struck Midway Atoll with fighters and divebombers attacking the seaplane hangar, fuel tanks, mess hall, gallery and command post on Sand Island. The powerhouse on Eastern Island also suffered slight damage, though, as much of Midway was comprised of underground bunkers, most of the bombs had little effect. The U.S. Marines attempted to defend the island with twenty-seven Brewster Buffalo fighters, the American counterpart to the Japanese Zero fighter. Only seven Buffalos survived, and those incurred severe damage. Of the three runways on Eastern Island, two were destroyed. The Japanese left the remaining one intact in hopes of utilizing it for their own purposes in the future.

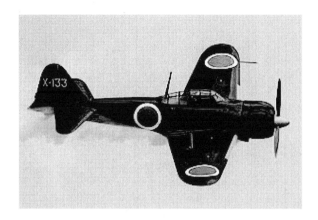

Mitsubishi A6M3 Zero Model.

For the first two hours, we were definitely losing the battle. As earlier stated, the marines lost twenty of their twenty-seven Brewster Buffalo fighters. This was in addition to our torpedo bombers annihilated by Japanese antiaircraft fire and their Zero fighters. The U.S.S. *Hornet* launched thirty torpedo bombers, and only one plane survived, the *Ensign Gay.* They then launched fifteen more aircraft, and only four of those survived. So out of forty-five aircraft, we lost forty. But the tide was about to turn.

U.S.S. Hornet *Torpedo Bomber.*

Rear Admiral Clarence Wade McClusky, Jr., USN.
1902 – 1976. Official U.S. Navy Photograph, from the collections of the
Naval Historical Center.

Three squadrons of SBD Dauntless divebombers led by Lieutenant Commander Wade McClusky had been searching for the Japanese forces for two hours. Despite running low on fuel, McClusky pressed on, and only moments later he spotted the white wake of a fast-moving Japanese destroyer. McClusky told his men, "That destroyer has to be racing to join the main fleet. We will follow it." Only moments later they found three Japanese aircraft carriers.

SBD Dauntless Dive Bombers.

Flying patrol has been defined as, "Endless hours of boredom punctuated by brief moments of sheer terror!" A major portion of any VP squadron's operations was maritime patrol – monotonous visual search of the sea's surface for the one white can which could be a submarine periscope feather. Breathlessly hot in the tropics and achingly cold in the Arctic, the PBY was at-one hated and loved. For, the rugged old P-boat, in spite of her shortcomings, rarely failed to bring her crew home in spite of all that the enemy or the weather could muster to bring her down. (USN via Naval Institute)

Diving from twenty thousand feet and aided by the fact that the Japanese fighters were cruising at a low altitude in order to defend against torpedo planes, the dive bombers inflicted sufficient damage to sink all three carriers: the *Kagi*, the *Soryu* and the *Akagi*, the last of which was Admiral Nagumo's flagship and the pride of the Japanese empire.

They were aided by two factors. Following the strike on Midway, Admiral Nagumo had received word that the attack had caused only minimal damage, so he planned to rearm with bombs and strike the island again. Admiral Yamamoto responded that they would instead rearm with torpedoes and strike the American fleet. So when our dive bombers arrived, the Japanese were in the process of rearming, and their fighters were at a low altitude protecting their ships from our torpedo bombers.

Admiral Spruance conferred with Admiral Nimitz, characterizing the turn of events as a good day and wondering whether the destruction of three carriers was enough. Admiral Nimitz replied, "Hell no. I want the fourth carrier."

U.S. forces stalked and sank the fourth carrier, the *Hiryu*, but in turn suffered the loss of the *Yorktown*, an aircraft carrier.

Photo # 80-G-225341 Adm. Raymond A. Spruance, April 1944

Commander, Central Pacific Force, U.S. Pacific Fleet informal portrait photograph, taken 23 April 1944. Official U.S. Navy Photograph, now in the collections of the U.S. National Archives.

Late that afternoon, my PBY spotted a Japanese submarine attempting to submerge. All hatches were closed with no one on deck. We dropped the first bomb near the tail of the sub, and the second bomb right behind the conning tower. We made six circles, watching the debris surface.

On that day, I think we earned our pay. It was war, and I sure don't regret having sunk that sub, but the thought of what it must have been like for the crew still haunts me. Our bombs wouldn't likely have killed all the sailors aboard, but those left alive were doomed to sinking into the depths of the sea while the water rushed in. Flying during the war was dangerous as hell – in those years, we lost plenty of men when their planes, many of them untested designs, went down in the Pacific. But to me, serving in a tin can below the surface had to be worse.

By late afternoon, we had lost radio contact with Midway. Having no idea how our side had fared, we had an option to return to Midway or set down at sea. We dropped our two remaining bombs unarmed, set down at sea, and threw out a sea anchor. We floated all night, unaware of the day's results. It was the right thing to do, but in reality, if we had lost the battle, we had no good options. We didn't have enough fuel to escape to a safe base if we had lost Midway, so it was a long night of worry.

I grabbed my sleeping bag and climbed on top of the wing and strapped myself to the plane's antennae. I had just flown thirteen hours in the Battle of Midway Island. Having no idea whether our side was victorious, I fell into a paralyzing sleep. The next day, I would discover our fate and the fate of the American troops in one of the major turning points of World War II.

At sunrise, we finally made radio contact with Midway. To our relief, our side had emerged triumphant. Advised of a destroyer at the French Frigate Shoals loaded with aviation fuel, we took navigational sun shots, determined our position, and flew to the shoals. After refueling, we returned to Midway.

On June 5, we began the search for downed seamen. By late afternoon, one hundred miles north of Midway, we found a life raft with two men aboard, but we were running low on fuel, so we made contact with another VP-23 squadron PBY piloted by Bob Slater. He landed and picked up the men, Lieutenant Junior Grade Minuard Jennings and Ensign Humphrey Tallman from squadron VF-8.

Squadron VP-23 flew five rescue missions and saved eight men in the hours after the Battle of Midway. On June 6, I returned to Pearl Harbor and enjoyed five wonderful days at the Royal Hawaiian Hotel. It was a needed break after the recent battle, but soon enough I was back in the air.

On July 1, 1942, I was on my way to Noumea, New Caledonia, where we were tasked with patrolling over Guadalcanal and all of the Solomon Islands.

Those with limited knowledge of World War II may not recognize the significance of the Battle of Midway. Despite the relatively small amount of men and arms as compared to many other battles, it was arguably the most important battle of the war. Prior to this victory, the Japanese possessed naval superiority over the U.S. Afterwards, the adversaries became essentially equal and finally America could take the offensive. The combined military and psychological toll of the Doolittle raid and Midway on the Japanese turned the tide. There were still years of fighting ahead of us, but each island we captured was one step closer to an all-out invasion of the Japanese Home Islands. Every plane downed and ship sunk chipped away bit by bit at the Japanese sense of their military might. Month by month and battle by battle, as the war ground on, they became more and more desperate.

Upon being advised that the fourth and last Japanese carrier had been sunk during the Battle of Midway, Admiral Nimitz released the following message:

"To you who have participated in the Battle of Midway today, you have written a glorious page in our history. I am proud to be associated with you. I estimate that another day of all-out effort on your part will complete the defeat of the enemy."

Even as a participant at Midway, I could not foresee the stunning and overwhelming ramifications of the battle's outcome. Admiral Yamamoto had moved on Midway in order to draw out and destroy U.S. Pacific aircraft carrier forces. Admiral Yamamoto theorized that if Japan could destroy Midway's defenses and take the surrounding islands, they would have a critical strategic base from which to deny the United States access to much of the Pacific. The aptly named Midway Islands were located at the midpoint between Japan and Hawaii. Holding such a position could cripple the American Pacific Fleet.

Fortunately, Admiral Nimitz's superior communications intelligence afforded the United States the opportunity to ambush the Japanese. Had we lost Midway, the negative domino effect would have been fatal to our cause. For example, the 1942 Guadalcanal invasion would not have occurred, thus re-opening the Japanese threat to Australia. As a result, Australia would withdraw troops from North Africa. In all likelihood, Australia would have been neutralized and the American presence there eliminated. Hence, MacArthur's return to the Philippines would have been thwarted, and American submarines would not have Australian bases to disrupt Japanese shipping.

In that scenario, the Hawaiian Islands would have been exposed to invasion. The logical extension from there would be our western shores. With such threats to our homeland, the U.S. would have been compelled to curtail our European forces. The implications of a loss at Midway are mind-boggling.

Regarding Midway, Winston Churchill stated, "This memorable American victory was of cardinal importance, not only to the United States but to the whole allied cause...At one stroke, the dominant position of Japan in the Pacific was reversed." In a more chilling description of events, Admiral Halsey said that, had we lost Midway, it would have prolonged the war many months, and a loss of Midway coupled with a loss of Guadalcanal would have been a real threat to winning the war.

Military historians have called the Battle of Midway "the greatest naval battle of all time." I am happy to say I played a small part in it.

Guadalcanal and Admiral Bull Halsey

After the Pearl Harbor attack, I not only participated in the Battle of Midway Island, but also the battles for Marshall and Gilbert, Tulagi, Santa Cruz, Renault, Stewart and Savo Islands.

Guadalcanal played an integral part in the war, as the series of islands in the vicinity would act as stopping points between Japan and the United States. That area in the South Pacific contained innumerable small islands. Some were inhabited, others were not. In order to effectively wage war, the planes had to hop from island to island in order to refuel.

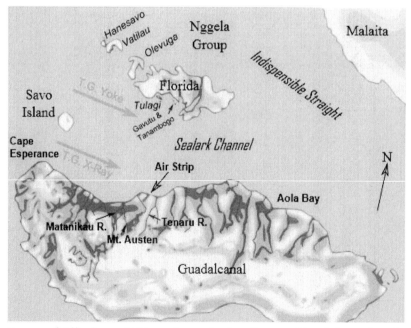

Routes of Allied amphibious forms for landing on Guadalcanal and Tulgai, 7 August, 1942.

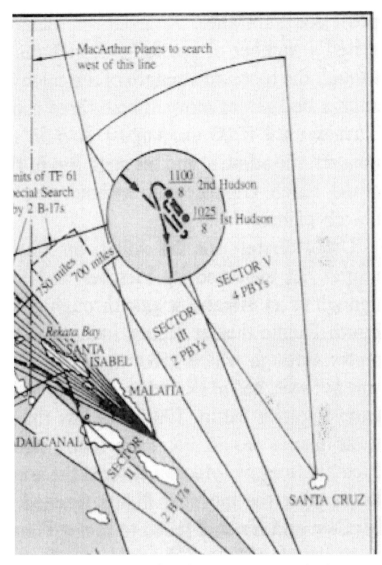

Mikawa's Approach and McCain's Air-Search Plan.

On July 1, 1942, our squadron VP-23 moved to Noumea, New Caledonia, and began anti-submarine patrol over Guadalcanal and all the Solomon Islands. New Caledonia was a beautiful place. Its English name was given by the explorer James Cook in 1774, and since 1853 it had been under French control. For a farm boy from Texas, places like Hawaii and New Caledonia were like paradise.

I didn't get to experience as much of the islands as I would have liked, because after Midway, our forces were pressing our advantage, committed to rooting Japanese troops out on every island they had dug in.

Our flight crew consisted of eight men, five of whom were enlisted. I spent every fifth night aboard the aircraft. We always had someone aboard to watch for attacks and to make sure the plane was ready at a moment's notice. For six months I patrolled over and around Guadalcanal. Only twenty-five miles in diameter, Guadalcanal rests 3,500 miles southwest of Pearl Harbor and 600 miles from Australia. It was a key strategic island. If we didn't take it, the Japanese could threaten Australia and use it to stage another attack on Hawaii.

Vice Admiral Richard Ghormley was the commander of all the Guadalcanal forces. The vice admiral had a reputation as a planner who kept his eyes open and his mouth shut. But he had never actually been on the island. Things were bleak, and we were definitely losing the battle in the South Pacific. Despite the success at Midway, the Japanese still held a number of islands that served as a protective circle around their territories. They had driven the British out of what is now Malaysia, American forces out of the Philippines, and the Dutch out of Indonesia. If we couldn't take Guadalcanal and the other Japanese island bases, our Pacific allies would be under threat of Japanese attacks, and we couldn't advance toward Japan to end the war.

On October 15, 1942, Ghormley sent a letter of resignation to Admiral Nimitz. It read, in part, "My forces are totally inadequate to meet this situation." Nimitz believed Ghormley to be an intelligent and dedicated officer, but not tough enough to face this crisis. He accepted the resignation and found a man he thought capable of the kind of bold action needed to push the Japanese back toward their Home Islands.

Photo # 80-G-12864-A   Vice Admiral Robert L. Ghormley in 1942

Vice Admiral Robert L. Ghormley. Official U.S. Navy Photograph, now in the collections of the National Archives.

In October 1942, Admiral Nimitz sent Admiral Halsey to relieve Ghormley. "Bull" Halsey embodied the stereotype of a street brawler, a man who craved action. His reputation as a no-nonsense, strapping and resilient character fit the bill. Nimitz knew we weren't going to think or plan our way to victory, so he chose someone who had no patience for endless analysis. Bull Halsey was a man who was ready at any moment to jump into a fight, and that's just what the Pacific theater needed.

Admiral Halsey immediately moved my squadron to Espirito Santo, which was three hundred miles closer to Guadalcanal. Halsey visited every unit on the island and told the troops, "We will no longer allow the enemy to call the shots. We will take command, and we will kill every son of a bitch on this island and I will be right there with you."

Halsey came aboard the U.S.S. *Curtiss*, my ship at the time, and I had the distinct pleasure of shaking his hand. This man instilled a fighting spirit in me, and in all of the men he led. We didn't know then how we were going to start calling the shots, but after meeting Halsey, I knew he'd come up with a way.

The *Curtiss* was a seaplane tender, which provided facilities for operating seaplanes. It had sustained damage during the attack on Pearl Harbor after a divebomber dove into one of its topside cranes and other Japanese bombs exploded, causing damage in the engine room. The *Curtiss* lost twenty men at Pearl Harbor. Still, after just one month of repairs, it was completely mended and went on to serve our squadron.

Photo # NH 97415   USS Curtiss off San Diego, California, circa later 1940s or early 1950s

U.S.S. Curtiss (AV-4) off San Diego, California, during the later 1940s or early 1950s. Official U.S. Navy Photograph, from the collections of the Naval Historical Center.

Fleet Admiral William Frederick Halsey, Jr., USNR 1882 – 1959. Official U.S. Navy Photograph, from the collections of the Naval Historical Center.

I consider Admiral "Bull" Halsey my hero. I believe Halsey and the infamous General George Patton could have been brothers. They thought and acted alike, and God help us, we need more like them. Halsey wasn't just a brave and brilliant strategist; he also had a way with words.

In the early 1930s Americans sold scrap iron like crazy, and the Japanese were buying it. While passing a San Francisco shipyard and spotting a Japanese freighter being loaded, Halsey said to his son, "We will get this back in the form of bullets."

Emperor Hirohito of Japan famously rode a beautiful white stallion. At the beginning of the war, Halsey said, "I will ride that son of a bitch down Main Street in Tokyo."

Early in the Pacific conflict, Halsey visited General MacArthur and told him "You are smart, General, but you are glory happy, and we need to work together to end this conflict."

After the war, MacArthur said, "The Pacific Ocean without Halsey will never be the same; it will just be another ocean."

From 1941 to 1945, Admiral Halsey commanded the task force centered on the carrier U.S.S. *Enterprise* in a series of raids against Japanese-held targets. He was made commander, South Pacific Area, and led the Allied forces over the course of the Battle for Guadalcanal (1942–43) and the fighting up the Solomon chain (1942–45). In 1943 he was made commander of the Third Fleet, the post he held through the duration of hostilities.

Photo # 19-N-89185 USS Enterprise in Puget Sound, Sept. 1945

U.S.S. Enterprise. Photograph from the Bureau of Ships Collection in the U.S. National Archives.

Just prior to the Battle of Midway, Halsey lay in the Pearl Harbor Naval Infirmary suffering from a severe case of shingles. Halsey remarked, "The greatest sea battle of all time is about to take place and here I am taking baths in oatmeal."

Nimitz came to Halsey upon his promotion inquiring who could take his place on the *Enterprise*. Halsey recommended Rear Admiral Raymond Spruance.

In disbelief, Nimitz replied, "Hell, he's a cruiser commander."

Halsey backed up his choice, stating, "Yes, but he runs them fast enough to stay up with my carriers."

Leading Allied naval forces to victory in the Guadalcanal Campaign, his ships remained at the leading edge of the Admiral Nimitz's "island-hopping" campaign through 1943 and early 1944. In June 1944, Halsey was given command of the U.S. Third Fleet. That September, his ships provided cover for the landings on Peleliu before embarking on a series of damaging raids on Okinawa and Formosa (now Taiwan). In late October, the Third Fleet was assigned to provide cover for the landings on Leyte and to support Vice Admiral Thomas Kinkaid's Seventh Fleet.

Resuming command in late May, Halsey made a series of carrier attacks against the Japanese Home Islands. During this time, he again sailed through a typhoon, though no ships were lost. A court of inquiry recommended that he be reassigned; however, Nimitz overruled the judgment and allowed Halsey to retain his post. Halsey's last attack came on August 13, 1945, and he was present aboard the U.S.S. *Missouri* when the Japanese surrendered on September 2, 1945.

En route to Guadalcanal after being assigned command in a four-engine U.S. Navy flying boat, Admiral Halsey's pilot received a warning that a squadron of Japanese Zeros had just left the island. Halsey ordered the pilot to alter the course and head to Noumea, New Caledonia, immediately. Admiral Halsey foiled the Japanese spies who had reported his departure from Pearl Harbor. They knew this type of aircraft would carry important personnel. Halsey was no one's fool.

Fortunately, Admiral Halsey made it safely to base and immediately put his personal stamp on the operations. He seized the headquarters, which Ghormley had never visited, ordered the officers to remove their ties, and moved the fleet from Auckland to Noumea. Admiral Halsey strutted into our unit and every unit on the island.

When I met Admiral Halsey, he lived up to the legend. In the brief period that he addressed our unit, he instilled a confidence and courage in each of us. He liked to repeat his famous slogan, "Hit hard, hit fast, hit often." Most importantly, he made us a promise that he was in the fight with us, and he was.

Admiral Halsey's arrival unquestionably bolstered our morale at a critical juncture. No one should underestimate the degree to which confidence guides the outcome of any contest. Guadalcanal was no exception.

My six-month campaign in Guadalcanal consisted of seven naval engagements, dozens of clashes and daily aerial combat.

Lockheed P-38 Fighters.

At that time, U.S. intelligence learned of Admiral Yamamoto's presence in Guadalcanal and discovered the details of his planned departure. As soon as his aircraft was airborne, our Marine Corps arrived with eight Lockheed P-38 fighters and shot his plane down. I had the immense pleasure of witnessing this glorious moment while flying some six thousand feet overhead when his plane hit the water. We knew he would never return to his flower gardens.

During my six-month deployment at Guadalcanal, I flew forty-eight missions over Tulagi, Santa Cruz, Renault, the Marshal and Gilberts, and the Stewart and Savo Islands. We had many encounters with Japanese Zeroes, and often landed with an aircraft full of holes. On two occasions, we returned on one engine. Fortunately, both times we were close to home base, because a PBY does not perform well on one engine. We never had the pleasure of sinking a sub at Guadalcanal, but we did report many Japanese ship locations and movements. Many of those ships never made it back to Japan.

Following Pearl Harbor, the Navy's enlisted pilots became officers. My pilot, Lieutenant J.G. Murphy, stood among the greatest of pilots in the Pacific theater. On October 16, 1942, while patrolling two hundred miles northeast of Espirito Santo, we were jumped by a Japanese Zero fighter. At the time, our aircraft patrolled the area from four thousand feet.

When the Zero initially appeared, we descended to skim the water, thus eliminating the Zero's ability to circle us and fire from all angles. His second approach came from the port side. Our port-side waist gunner scored a number of shots, causing the Zero to emit smoke. But the Zero's shots took a toll on our port engine and we were also trailing smoke. On his third run at us, he shot across the wing section, barely missing the fuel tanks. Ultimately, his ammunition only made contact with the trailing edges of the wing, only four feet from my office in the conning tower. After that third attempt, the Zero gave up.

The attack left us 150 miles from Espirito Santo trailing oil from the left engine. Looking at the gauge, I reported that we had less than a gallon of oil remaining. Holes dotted the left side of the aircraft and the port engine. We limped back home, making it only due to the skill of Lieutenant Murphy. That man could land a flying bus in a backyard pool, that's how good he was.

Two days later, with the holes in the aircraft patched, a new oil tank installed, and other repairs made, we were back on patrol. We often landed with a plane that was unfit to fly. The ground crews were amazing. They could repair and refit a shot-up plane in just a day or two and get us back in the air. There were many unrecognized heroes in my war, and the guys that kept the planes flying are at the top of the list in my opinion.

We ran across plenty of Zeroes while on patrol, and men often talked about how dangerous the aircraft and how skilled their pilots were. In my experience, the reputation of the Japanese pilots as the best and the bravest is exaggerated. Although some of them may have been exceptional, I certainly encountered plenty who turned tail and ran when our waist hatch gunners would raise the canopy to expose a .50 caliber machine gun. Later on, after many of their best pilots and planes had been shot down, the Japanese developed the kamikaze attack, in which the plane was a flying bomb and the pilot would steer it directly at ships, but those tactics were not employed during the early part of the conflict. As a tactic, as terrifying as it was, it was a mark of desperation, and when the Japanese adopted it, we knew we had them on the run.

We were in that war to win: the Japanese had pulled off a cowardly sneak attack, and we were out for revenge. We wanted to shoot down and bomb as many of them as we could find. Another motivator in our fight was the Japanese reputation for cruelty. The Japanese military enjoyed brutality. They used every device known to mankind as a means of torture. The Japanese cut off prisoners' fingers to retrieve a ring; fed them dead rats; tied prisoners prior to beating them; placed tourniquets around men's penises to cause their bladders to burst; and forced prisoners to drink their own urine and eat their own feces. For that, we wanted to kill them, and for certain we were afraid of being captured.

By January 1, 1943, U.S. forces completely controlled Guadalcanal. Part of my squadron had orders to return to Pearl Harbor but to leave the planes behind. Nothing about the voyage approached luxury. In order to gain passage on the U.S. naval freighter bound for Hawaii, we had to first unload the vessel. Once aboard, we had fresh drinking water, but not a drop for any other use. I recommend neither shaving nor bathing with salt water. Fortunately, a rainstorm during the voyage provided us with our only immersion in fresh water the whole trip.

European Theatre

Our return to Pearl Harbor began a series of changing directives. We were to travel to San Diego, commission a new squadron of PBYs, and return to the South Pacific. The heavy cruiser U.S.S. *Detroit* transported us to San Diego, where our orders changed. Now, we began training in the first PB4Ys, the naval designation for the B-24 bomber.

Dunkeswell, Devonshire, England

With the new B-24s, we formed squadron VB-103. After a month we transferred to Newfoundland for two more months of training. After that, I had a fifteen-day leave of absence. I headed back to Texas to visit my parents. I can tell you, they were darn glad to see me, and I was just as happy to see them. When I had joined up just a few years before, I was good and tired of Texas. But after years of dangerous duty in far foreign lands, I can't tell you how glad I was to see our farm again.

On April 1, 1943, the Navy transferred us to Dunkeswell, Devonshire, England, approximately a hundred miles from London. I was in the European theater for fifteen months, patrolling the English Channel and the Bay of Biscay on the western coast of France. During patrol, enlisted crewmen were required to wear the Royal Air Force uniform with an American flag sewn unto the left shoulder. The Navy-enlisted chambray shirt and jeans were not considered uniform. If captured, we knew we would be executed as spies, since we were not in American uniforms.

Our crew consisted of eleven men: the pilot, co-pilot, navigator, plane captain, bombardier, two radiomen, two waist gunners, a tail turret gunner and a tunnel hatch gunner. I acted as the plane captain and top turret gunner.

The PB4Y had no pressurization and therefore no heat. We wore electrically heated suits that rarely worked, and ten thousand feet above the English Channel was quite brisk. These early-model PB4Ys had two .50 caliber machine guns in the nose, which could not be used effectively. Later models had better nose guns, but before then, German fighter pilots quickly recognized the limitations of the fore .50s and attacked the PB4Y head-on. We lost two aircraft due to this deficiency.

Also, the fuel panel was located behind the bomb bay and up over the center section of the wing called the fuel transfer panel. As the plane captain and top turret gunner, it was my responsibility to climb up to the wing during flight and physically change the hose connection to transfer fuel. This was at best an inconvenient task, and under fire dangerous and often almost impossible. The later model corrected both of these defects.

PB4Y-1. Official U.S. Navy Photograph, from the collections of the Naval Historical Center.

When I wasn't in the air, I lived in a round metal Quonset hut in Dunkeswell along with the members of my crew and another flight crew. During my one seven-day leave, I visited London and experienced Buckingham Palace, Big Ben, the changing of the guard and even some nightclubs. The people I met were wonderful, and grateful for America's efforts in the European theater. I wish I had had more time to get to know England, but my primary English experience consisted of patrolling the area.

A Dunksewell communal site showing the muddy conditions that existed at the base throught the spring and winter months.

I am sure many readers have heard of the German "buzz bomb." It was a small, unmanned airplane powered by a small gasoline engine carrying a small bomb. The aircraft was fueled with just enough gas to get it to the prescribed destination. When it ran out of fuel, it plumetted to earth. In 1943, they were continually flying over London and dropping onto the city. America has never been invaded or attacked on a daily basis by another country, so it's hard for many of us to imagine the terror of a constant and sustained bombing campaign. The British, in my experience, never gave into fear, and they never complained.

In 1940 alone, over a million homes in London were destroyed. Homeless survivors were shifted to still-standing homes, and the entire country pulled together, refusing to give up despite the daily attacks. During my seven-day leave to see London, the natives told me when you heard the engine of a buzz bomb stop, you had better find cover. They were a brave and hospitable people, despite that their capital was being attacked every day.

While on patrol, we regularly encountered German Messerschmitt 109s and Fokker III fighter aircraft. Upon discovery of one of these aircraft, we had the choice to fight or dive into the clouds for cover. Occasionally, the cloud-protection strategy would fail and a German fighter would be waiting on the other side of the cloud.

The number of WW-II
Quonset huts produced
were as followed:

T-rib Quonset   8,200

Quonset Huts. Photo from Seebee Museum and Memorial Park.

We returned from many flights with a perforated fuselage, three engines, and injured crewman, but in my plane we never had a crewman killed.

I survived fifty-six missions over the channel and the bay. We were lucky: the average tour of duty was twenty-five missions, and the chance of surviving those missions was only one in four.

Jack Holder's Squadron (Jack is kneeling, first row, left).

I had the pleasure of shooting down one German Messerschmitt 109 fighter. We had just emerged from the cloud cover when the 109 crossed in front of us. Without even time to reposition the gun turret, I instinctively pressed the two triggers and watched as the 109 exploded. Relief, adrenaline and joy shot through my body.

German Messerschmitt 109 Fighter. From War History Online.

My aircraft was No. 3, and was named *Calverts & Coke*. In my younger years, I had had a few drinks of Calverts and Coca-Cola. When we returned from this flight, there was a bottle of champagne waiting to celebrate the mission and the downing of the Messerschmitt, and we also had a few Calverts.

Lone patrol of Calvert & Coke, an early model PB4Y. By early 1944, most Liberators with the Plexiglas nose and the free-swinging machine guns were replaced by aircraft equipped with the ERCO bow turret.

On one occasion, I received credit for a kill of a German submarine. Another PB4Y crew joined us in making two runs over it as it surfaced.

We each dropped two one-thousand-pound bombs. Diving on an enemy sub through a hail of anti-aircraft and machine gun fire was something like Christmas and the Fourth of July combined, all lights and color, but surviving the attack was far too early to begin the celebration. Celebration came after you had returned to your home base, and in this case it was a joyous affair.

This was my PB4Y-1 aircraft No. 3, also known as Calverts & Coke. Left to right: Jack Holder (Plane Captain), Dave Emmons (Radio Man Second Class), Howard Perkins (Radio Man First Class). Dunkeswell, Devonshire, England, 1943.

Christmas 1943, Dunkeswell, Devonshire, England.

This was a Christmas tree in our Quonset hut for sixteen Navy PB4Y crewmen. A keg of beer and a wall full of stockings.

I transferred to Chincoteague, Virginia, in July of 1944 after flying twice the usual number of missions over the English Channel. I was awarded a Distinguished Flying Cross for meritorious service for antisubmarine patrol over the English Channel. I received a second Distinguished Flying Cross for sinking the submarine. I liked getting those medals just fine, but mostly I was happy to be back home. Flying in those days, particularly in the Pacific theater, was dangerous. Overall during the war, 43,000 planes and their men were lost, 23,000 of those in combat. Almost half of the lost planes and men were due to accidents and to the fact that most of the aircraft we flew were new and largely untested. I got two medals, but anyone who made it home after years of flying in that war is a hero in my book.

When Fleet Wing Seven ceased operations from Dunkeswell, the squadroms had flown a total of 6,464 mussions, sunk five submarines, and assisted in sinking of at least four others.

Jack Receiving the Distinguish Flying Cross, 1946.

Following are the contents of the letter I received from the Secretary of the Navy:

THE SECRETARY OF THE NAVY
WASHINGTON

The President of the United States takes pleasure in presenting the

DISTINGUISHED FLYING CROSS TO

JOSEPH NORMAN HOLDER

AVIATION MACHINISTS MATE FIRST CLASS

UNITED STATES NAVY

for service set forth in the following;

CITATION:

For heroism and extraordinary achievement in aerial flight as an Air crewman of a United States Naval Patrol Bomber Plane in Anti-Submarine operations in the Day of Biscay and the Western Approaches to the United Kingdom from April 1,1943 to June 25, 1944. Completing his 56th mission during this period, HOLDER contributed materially to the success of his squadron. His courage and devotion to duty were in keeping with the highest traditions of the United States Naval Service.

For the President,

James Forrestal

Copy to; Secretary of the Navy

Public Relations Navy Dept.

Ref;Bdawds Serial 925 of 7 Dec 46

Send Medal

Transposed letter of Distinguished Flying Cross notification, December 7, 1946

My assignment in Virginia was to assist in training a new PB4Y squadron. The European conflict was winding down, so in the end the new squadron was not commissioned. I remained in Virginia for ten months as plane captain. While I was there, I met a shipmate by the name of Paul Honaker, who was a first-class aviation mechanic. He became one of the best friends I have ever had, and we spent most of our liberty time together. He had a green 1937 Ford, which never started without a lot of work. I kept the rear of that car polished with my bare hands, and we probably pushed that thing for as many miles as we drove it.

My next transfer took me to a PB4Y-2 squadron in Pensacola, Florida, where I continued to serve as plane captain. The PB4Y-2 was the Navy's version of the B-24. The aircraft featured a single-tail surface, larger and more powerful engines and increased speed.

Navy PB4Y Squadron VB-103 crewmen, Distinguished Flying Cross presentation, Chincoteague, Virginia, 1944. Left to right: James Oliver AOM1/C, Jerry John AMM1/C, Robert Stelzer AOM1/C, Jack Holder AMM1/C, H.D. Roberts AOM2/C.

I was married November 6, 1945. My father sent me a $100 dollar bill. Today that would've been $1200. This was not a happy marriage. When I joined the Navy, I was a twenty-year or possibly a thirty-year man. I planned to leave the Navy, no less than a Chief Warrant Officer, but my wife talked me into getting a discharge. This was my first mistake. Secondly, following my Union Oil Company plane crash, she wanted me to stop flying. This was my second mistake. I gave up the two things in life that I wanted most.

The war finally ended on September 2, 1945, and boy were we happy. Despite that the conflict had ended, I was still in the service, and the Navy had plenty of work for me to do. In October 1946, I transferred to a Naval R5D Transport Squadron in Patuxent River, Maryland. I was designated as a plane captain. The commercial realm knew the R5D aircraft as the Douglas DC-4. It was one of the main aircraft that made up the fleets of most commercial airlines in the 1940s and early 1950s.

Navy R5D Commercial DC4.

Finally, after a turbulent seven years, ten months and five days, I honorably departed the service of the United States Navy. Aside from the experiences I had had that turned a Texas farm boy into a man who had seen much of the world, I emerged with several commendations and awards: two Distinguished Flying Crosses, six Air Medals, an American Defense Medal, an American Campaign Medal, a European African Middle Eastern Campaign Medal, an Asiatic Pacific WWII Campaign Medal, a Presidential Unit Citation, a Combat Action Commemorative, a Combat Service Commemorative, an Airborne and Assault Commemorative, an Overseas Service Commemorative, a Navy Commemorative, an Honorable Service Commemorative, two Good Conduct Medals, six Meritorious Citations signed by the Secretary of the Navy, and one Citation signed by the President of the United States.

Post WWII

THE U.S. NAVY AWARDED ME an honorable discharge as an aviation machinist mate first class on March 5, 1948 in Washington, D.C.

I moved immediately to Dallas, Texas. Braniff International Airways offered me a position as an apprentice mechanic, and after what I had been through, being an "apprentice" was no difficulty. Soon, I rose up the ranks, and each year yielded a promotion. Within two years, I was a master mechanic. In addition to a good job after the war, Braniff afforded me the opportunity to obtain my Commercial Flight Engineer Certificate.

I moved to California for an aircraft mechanic position with Northrop Aircraft. I lived near Hawthorne Airport, but in the end, the job was tedious. I had spent so much time flying that being stuck on the ground would never satisfy me any longer. After a couple of months, I peered across the runway and saw the insignia of my old company, Braniff, plastered across two DC-4 aircraft. My curiosity piqued, I strolled across the runway and met Kirk Kerkorian, the owner of the aircraft and of the Los Angeles Air Services (LAAS), a non-scheduled charter airline.

An Armenian multi-billionaire, Kerkorian was instrumental in developing what was once a dusty desert town into the ritzy, glitzy Las Vegas. His legend originates from his development of famous Las Vegas hotels such as the Hilton and the original MGM Grand. He also owned the Metro-Goldwyn-Mayer film studio, among other endeavors.

Three years my senior, the feisty billionaire still played tennis when he was ninety-six, and at that age drove himself to his Las Vegas office in a Jeep. At one point he became entangled in an infamous paternity suit, and while he was exonerated, he still gave the child a ten-million-dollar trust for when he reached the age of eighteen. Kirk was a good man, and though he owned a number of high-profile businesses, he liked to keep a low profile. He never allowed anything to be named after him, no matter how much money he had donated to a cause. With much sadness, I have to say my good friend Mr. Kirk Kerkorian died in July 2015.

Kerkorian took a liking to me right off the bat when I walked into the LAAS office that day, and he immediately hired me as a flight engineer. This meeting began years of a positive, professional relationship. I still have fond memories of watching Kirk walk around the casino floors followed by an attendant carrying a bag of silver dollars. Despite giving up high-stakes gambling years before, he still liked to dabble in dollar slots.

I had operated aircraft for years, but the company grounded me in May 1952 when Kerkorian required that the flight engineers acquire pilot's licenses. Kerkorian wanted the engineers to have the ability to double as the co-pilot in case of an emergency. My previous flying experiences had not mandated a license, and since I didn't have one, I was out. I wasn't done flying, so I knew it was time to formally get my license.

I focused on getting back to the air and purchased a small disassembled aircraft, a Luscombe-Silvaire.

I rented an eighteen-wheel flatbed truck to transport the plane the twenty miles to the hangar at Hawthorne Airport. Restoring the dilapidated plane necessitated a general overhaul of the engine in addition to re-covering the wings and other adjustments. My concentrated efforts returned the plane to airworthiness in record time, enabling me to begin training in the aircraft during flight school.

Jack's aircraft 1950: Luscombe-Silvaire. Hawthorne, California.

I arrived early to work, where I acted as an aircraft mechanic in the interim. I flew before work, during my lunch break and again after work. By cramming in triple sessions daily, I had my Commercial Pilot Certification and an Instrument Rating within six months. I soloed on a Sunday morning, and Kerkorian made a special trip to the airport to watch my flight. LAAS reinstated me as a co-pilot, and Jack Holder was back in the air.

The LAAS schedule consisted of mainly chartered flights that varied the routes and times from one day to the next. One month my assignment could be a flight to Germany, the next to Japan. What my schedule lacked in consistency was made up for by the excitement.

I lived in various parts of L.A. from 1950 to the 1960s: Gardenia, Inglewood and eventually Westchester. Westchester bordered the L.A. International Airport, and I frequented a spot called the Bar of Melody.

The Bar of Melody was only two miles from the airport and attracted plenty of airline personnel. It was a dark, dramatic venue that attracted intrigues and exploits. Its colorful owner, James Marion, often infamously plied his customers with free drinks before suggesting a whirlwind trip to Vegas.

James's epic gambling earned him a regular account in downtown Vegas. On one fateful excursion, an alcohol-soaked Jim was up when a less intoxicated companion managed to drag him to the airport. Their flight back to L.A. was delayed, so Jim finagled his way back to the casino. By the time his friend got him on a flight back, Jim had managed to squander his winnings plus another fifteen thousand.

Shortly afterward, Jim entered his bar to find two men in black suits sitting at the bar. The ominous gentlemen informed Jim in no uncertain terms that he had until 4:00 pm the next day to shell out the fifteen grand or hand over the deed to the bar. Jim managed to save the bar and ultimately his marriage by ending the treks to Vegas.

My own Bar of Melody brush with adventure began as I innocently enjoyed a cocktail at the bar. Ralph Waldron, an employee of Garrett Air Research Manufacturing Company, bellied up and sat next to me. Eventually, Ralph and I moved to a more secluded table in the restaurant. He revealed that he worked with the CIA.

He told me, "We will deposit ten thousand dollars in the bank of your choice. All you have to do is fly to Havana and drop leaflets. When you return, you will find another ten thousand in your account."

This trip was to be made in a Mitchell B-25 bomber. I considered this for some time, but my level-headedness overcame my reckless side. I decided that the chances were pretty good that Castro would prevent my return flight from Cuba to Miami. I declined.

Meanwhile, I thrived in my new job. I enjoyed shuttling soldiers from Japan to San Francisco, flying new automobile hardware from Detroit to Long Beach during a freight line strike, and the thrill of undertaking a unique task each day. One assignment during the 1956 Hungarian Revolt entailed transporting Hungarian refugees from

Munich to New York. These frightened refugees boarded the plane each clutching a small loaf of bread and a small bottle of water. After much cajoling, the flight attendants finally convinced the refugees that they would be fed. The refugees were used to taking care of themselves and not expecting much, and it took them some time to believe someone might give them something simply out of kindness.

In March 1957, I received a call from Kerkorian's secretary informing me that my boss had sold all of LAAS's aircraft and the company was out of business.

Although I was disappointed, I would not be unemployed long. Union Oil Company of California ran an ad for an aircraft pilot. After an interview with the chief pilot and vice president of the aviation department, I had a position as a co-pilot before the end of the month.

Union Oil DC3, 1958. Jack is in middle front.

My new company had four airplanes all based in Burbank, California. The small fleet was comprised of a Twin Beech C-52, a DC-3 and two Convairs: a 340 and a 440. The flights took us to many places. Some frequently visited locales included Calvary, Platte River and Yellowknife, Canada, as well as Newark, San Francisco, Lower California, La Paz, Jamaica and Houston.

Unlike many corporate aviation departments, Union Oil flights were scheduled just like an airline. We had a CEO and board chairman who came from U.S. Steel, and he made this schedule work. He made frequent trips to New York.

Union Oil Convair 580.

In early 1960, Pacific Aeromotive Company (PAC) converted the two Convairs from reciprocating engines to prop jets. The conversion changed them into machines that could fly 350 miles per hour and had a range of 2900 miles.

On December 23, 1963, we had a scheduled trip from Houston, Texas, to Midland Odessa, Texas. We were taking a Union Oil vice president, Ray Burke, to his parents' home to spend Christmas. Much of Texas was under a severe weather storm. Ice covered the trees and highways. The roads were particularly impassable.

We approached Midland Odessa without incident. However, during the descent from 18,000 feet and upon reaching 7000 feet, we entered the overcast and encountered freezing rain. On this leg of the trip, the chief pilot was flying the aircraft and I acted as co-pilot. On the return trip to Burbank, California, the pilot and I would swap roles and I would act as pilot.

As the co-pilot, my duties included de-icing the wing and tail sections. The job can be tricky, as it entails removing ice from the aircraft's leading edge surfaces by applying heated air, which is derived from the jet engine compressor at 360 degrees Fahrenheit. If the heat were left on too long, it could warp the leading edge surfaces. I could see that no ice had formed on the leading edge surfaces of the wings, but I could not see the tail.

The descent from 7000 to 2000 feet went smoothly. But when the approach flaps were made at twenty degrees, the aircraft began to lose elevation control. During the final approach with forty-degree flaps applied, the nose dropped. The aircraft nose gear hit the first light standard and sheared the gear. After we lost the nose gear, the aircraft hit nose first and skidded down the runway 975 feet, engulfed in flames. I was knocked unconscious.

Jack's accident, December 1963.

I came to and found myself still strapped in by the seatbelt despite the seat's detachment from the floor of the plane. Unstrapping myself from the seat, I searched for a way out. Flames consumed the cabin. Desperate for an escape route, my only opportunity appeared to be the direct vision windows on either side of the cockpit. The windows measured a mere ten by twelve inches, as they only existed to enable the pilots to gain visibility in situations where the windscreen freezes over. I frantically tried to squeeze through the window but could not pull my hips through the small space. The airplane's only passenger, Ray Burke, managed to wrench my trapped body through the window to safety.

Meanwhile, the captain remained ensnared in the cockpit of the flaming aircraft. All our efforts to save him failed. Finally, a Texas highway patrolman arrived after spotting the smoke from the plane. He grabbed an axe and rushed to the plane.

Desperately, he chopped a hole in the side of the cockpit and extracted the badly burned and still unconscious pilot. When the first firefighters arrived on scene, they discovered their truck had no chemicals necessary for extinguishing a fire that hot.

Ray Burke and the cabin boy fractured their ribs and were treated and released. The captain spent six weeks hospitalized for severe burns. I fractured several vertebrae as well as sustained multiple cuts, bruises and burns. After three weeks, the Midland Hospital released me with a back brace I would have to wear for six months.

The National Transportation Safety Board determined that no pilot error contributed to the crash. However, this did not convince the Union Oil vice president in charge of our aviation department. He hired an independent firm to further investigate the accident. The independent firm confirmed the lack of pilot error. Nonetheless, the company fired all personnel. The vice president's rationale was that any pilot who'd had a crash was more prone to have another.

Despite the unwarranted discharge, I remained undeterred. After a year of recuperating from the accident, I found a pilot position with Lockheed Aircraft. Unfortunately, I never felt satisfied with this position. Friends from Allied Signal reached out to me about a position with them. I moved on after only four months with Lockheed. My new endeavor took me back to Hawaii. My assignment entailed acting as the engineering service representative to Hawaiian and Aloha Airlines.

I spent one year as a field representative with Hawaiian Airlines until I was transferred to Braniff Airways in Dallas. After that it was off to London. It always made me happy to see London again, and in much better condition than I had seen it during the war. I spent five years there as a supervisor of field service engineers for BOAC and British European Airways.

In February 1975 I was transferred back to Phoenix for three years serving as a customer service engineer. I was not happy with the assignment so I left the company and moved to Hawkins, Texas, a small town thirty miles north of Tyler. I worked as an assistant golf pro for two years. I did not make a lot of money, but I had a lot of fun, as I had never lost my passion for golf. It was a bit odd to be out of the flying life; I had been involved with aircraft one way or another for thirty-five years at that point. I will say, though, that if a man can't fly regularly, playing golf every day goes a long way to making up for it.

Texco Oil Corporation

IN 1979, I FORMED A SMALL independent oil exploration company by the name of Texco. I was chairman and CEO with four partners. We drilled twenty-seven wells in Oklahoma, seven in Champaign, Illinois, three in Texas, and two in Louisiana. The third well we drilled in Okmulgee, Oklahoma, was a large gas well. We made the Tulsa, Oklahoma, headlines, which read: "Small Texas oil exploration co. makes huge gas discovery." During the late 1970s, investment money to drill a well was easy to find, and if the well was not productive, the investor could write it off.

In 1983, I received a call from a Texaco attorney, who advised me to cease and desist or Texaco would come after me for name infringement. I quickly changed the name to Onyx. That same year, the tax laws changed, and our investor could no longer write it off. For one year I kept my company alive with personal funds. I bought out my four partners, paid the lease on my office and paid four employees their salaries. In the end, I lost a lot of money. In 1984, I filed for corporate bankruptcy. I called my former boss at Allied Signal, told him the oil business had dried up, and that I needed a job. He said, "Come on in."

Allied Signal and Retirement

AFTER ONLY A PHONE CALL, Allied Signal decisively re-hired me as a mechanical engineer. I returned to Phoenix on April 1, 1984. The oil business behind me, I received a promotion to engineering manager and remained in that position until my retirement in December, 1991.

Some time after the death of my wife in 2010, my golfing buddies told me I needed to meet a lady to share my life with and that I could not continue without a companion. I was skeptical, as I had not been lucky in love the first time around, but when your friends corner you like that, you have to go along with them if only to be polite.

I went to a singles meeting and met a beautiful widowed lady, Ruth Calabro, who has become the treasure I wish I had met many years ago. I never really knew what love was until I met this wonderful person. At this writing, we have been together for five years, and we have a beautiful life together. I've worked hard my whole life, and more than that, I've always been lucky. I survived the war and came out of it with incredible experiences and marketable skills. I've had several careers, and most of them were exciting and satisfying. But I had never been lucky in love, and until I met Ruth, I had no idea what I had been missing.

Until I met Ruth, I never even told anyone I was a World War II veteran. I think that's common after people have served in difficult conflicts. I have many wonderful memories of my friends in the service and the experiences we had, but of course, there are as many or more

difficult memories, things I didn't care to think on much, and that I
never talked about.

I came home from the war mostly intact mentally and emotionally,
but I knew plenty of men who were plagued their whole lives by the
horrors they had experienced. Ruth convinced me to become involved
with other World War II veterans and tell my story. Since then, I have
given numerous presentations about my life, including my time in
the military. A little bit to my surprise, talking about my experiences
helped me a lot, and I hope that the events I have spoken at have
helped others who served too. One of the great things about giving
these talks was the opportunity to meet people who fought in World
War II, people who had had completely different experiences than
mine.

Navajo Code Talkers

In July 2014, I was invited by the Intel Corporation to present and to hear a presentation by the Navajo Code Talkers. A lot of World War II was fought behind the scenes. Of course the big moments like the Battle of Midway and the invasion of Normandy were important, but none of the major turning points of the war would have been possible without the efforts of our intelligence services. While I was hunting ships and subs, the intelligence people were fighting their own war, one that was most often a contest to break the enemy's codes.

In 1940, in the hope of putting into play a truly unbreakable code, a small group of Chippewa and Oneida Americans were added to the radio communications team of the 32nd Infantry Division. Later, when the need for combat radiomen who could accomplish absolutely secure communications was understood, men from the Sac and Fox tribes joined up.

Very few Americans spoke these indigenous languages, and in all the rest of the world, if there was anyone who could, we never found out about it. A Code Talker in the field could communicate sensitive information to another Code Talker in the rear and know that there was no way for the enemy to understand even a little of what they were saying.

I met a number of the surviving Code Talkers and enjoyed learning how the code was devised. Later that day, the men danced a traditional dance, something I had never seen. I felt honored to experience such a rare event, and it made me think again about how the war had brought the country together in many surprising ways.

Following their first dance, I was asked to give a presentation, and afterwards the Code Talkers asked me to join them in another dance.

Jack and Navajo Code Talkers Dance.

One of our dancers threw two one-dollar bills on the floor and we danced around them. Upon completion of the dance, one of the dancers picked them up and said, "Keep these for good luck."

I now have them in a frame with a picture of the group.

Grand Marshal For Veterans Day Parade

IN 2014, I WAS NOMINATED for the post of grand marshal by Brent Watkins, a friend from real estate school. Brent said, "Jack is an inspiration to me and many others that you are never too old to follow your dreams." I had never thought of it that way, but I think that's right: you never are too old to have a dream and go after it. My various careers and especially meeting Ruth is proof of that.

Veterans Day Parade, November 2014. Jack and Ruth.
Picture by Charles Gabrean.

This was a great honor for me and I will always remember the warm reception and the thousands of people that turned out for the parade to honor veterans of all our wars. Veterans are an odd bunch, in a way. Most of us don't talk about our service, and sometimes I think that leads people to forget how much it meant to us, how much our country means to us, and how much we sacrificed. A day like Veterans Day is a big deal; even though we don't talk about our service, being recognized for it once a year goes a long way toward making us feel like people do understand what we went through and that our experiences changed us.

Pearl Harbor: 73rd Anniversary

THROUGH THE GENEROSITY OF THE Chive Charities and the Greatest Generation Foundation, I was among twelve World War II veterans returning to Pearl Harbor in December, 2014.

The members attending were: George Norton, Thomas Petso, Michael M. Ganitch, Clarence Byal, Robert Addobati, Samuel Clower, Robert Blum, Victor Miranda, John C. Seelie, Edward Stone, Lawrence Parry and myself.

Twelve Pearl Harbor Survivors Traveling to Pearl Harbor for the 73rd Anniversary. Jack is number six from the right.

On Tuesday, December 2, I was aboard a Hawaiian Airlines jet bound for Hawaii. This was a seven-night all-expenses trip paid for by the Greatest Generation Foundation and all of their sponsors. We were treated like royalty. We stayed at the Hilton Hawaiian Village Waikiki Beach Resort, just three miles from downtown Honolulu.

I love going back to Hawaii. Yes, it holds difficult memories for me, but it's still one of the most magical places in this great and varied nation.

We were on the very tight schedule from 6:00 am until 9:00 pm, but what a glorious time we had. On Wednesday, December third, our first scheduled visit was the Hawaii Army Museum with Hawaiian school students. The war affected the whole country, but it will come as no surprise when I tell you that the people of the 50th state take it more seriously than most. If things had gone differently, it's likely that Hawaii wouldn't be a state at all, but just an outpost of the Japanese Empire. So when I spoke to students about the war in Hawaii, you bet they were paying close attention. There's a lot of pride in Hawaii, native pride, and pride at having resisted the Japanese attack, and kids there were more than willing to hear what I had to say.

Pearl Harbor 73rd Anniversary. December 2, 2014. Signing autographs at the Hilton Hawaiian Village.

National Memorial Cemetery of the Pacific.

My second engagement was a visit to the Punch Bowl National Cemetery. The cemetery is dedicated to those men and women that served in the United States Armed Forces. The walls of the memorial are etched with the names of those whose remains were never recovered from battle. It's a powerful monument. We lose men and women in war; that's the nature of war, and it's horrible. But to see the names of those who were never found – well, that hits me even harder. These people are truly lost, and we have only their names to remember them by.

Our third visit was a welcome reception at the world-famous Dukes in Waikiki for a wonderful dinner. My involvement with veterans' groups has been incredibly satisfying. I served my country during the war, and I'm proud of that. But the wonderful thing at my age is to have a chance to serve again by making sure that the value of service is not forgotten, and to have my efforts appreciated by so many.

On Thursday the fourth, our first stop was at Hickam Field Air Force Base. This base was named after the aviator pioneer Lieutenant

Colonel Horace Meek Hickam. Now, Hickam is the launch point of Strategic Air Mobility and Operational Missions in support of the global war on terrorism.

Hickman Field Air Force Base.

After Hickam, we went to the *Bowfin* Memorial. The U.S.S. *Bowfin* was a Balao-class submarine and was named after a voracious predatory fish native to the Great Lakes and the Mississippi valley.

Bowfin Memorial.

Next was a glorious private boat tour around Ford Island and a tour of the U.S.S. *Arizona* memorial, which is the resting place for the 1,102 of the 1,177 sailors killed on the *Arizona* during the attack on Pearl Harbor and Ford Island. The power of the *Arizona* memorial is hard to understand if you haven't visited it. It's one thing to celebrate someone's service by interring them in a military cemetery, and another thing entirely to allow them to rest where they fell. It's a true and honest testament to the horror of war and the ultimate sacrifice that is often demanded during a war.

U.S.S. Arizona Memorial.

On Friday, our first stop was Schofield Barracks and Wheeler Army Base. Each of us was assigned to a different classroom of young students. These children had prepared their classrooms with all types of greeting signs and thank-you messages for the presenters. They were so appreciative and respectful. It's sometimes tempting at my age to think of kids these days as having it too easy, but these kids understood that World War II was a turning point, and without the sacrifices that every American made back then, we might be living in a very different and worse country.

Wheeler Army Base children's classroom.

Next was the Marine Corps Base Hawaii ceremony with Wounded
Warriors. This was at Kaneohe bay. A group of young marines were
there recovering from their injuries, but they were all in good spirits
and so receptive. This kind of respect that crosses generational lines
is one of my favorite aspects of giving presentations to people in the
services. At ninety-two, I could talk to a twenty-year-old marine and
we had a connection that made age or the different wars we had fought
in unimportant. What we had in common was service, and sacrifice.
When you're very young, you crave respect from older people. And
when you're old, you feel some version of the same thing: you want the
younger generations to understand and appreciate you. A room full of
soldiers, old and young, is the answer to that need for understanding
and respect for someone like me. I met young men who had suffered
terrible wounds, and not one of them felt like their sacrifice was more
important than mine had been. It's true what they often say: having
served your country creates a brotherhood that can't be broken.

Lastly was the Chive Charities meeting late that afternoon. The
reception was sponsored by the Chive Charities president Mr. John

Resig. The reception was held on the open grounds of the Waikiki Hilton Hotel, with a crowd of more than five hundred guests treated in proper fashion and with fantastic food and drinks.

It so happened I was selected by our Greatest Generation Foundation President Mr. Timothy Davis to make the presentation for this crowd. This was such an honor, and when I received a standing ovation, well, that was something that I'll remember the rest of my life.

On December 6, there was a two-hour session of signing autographs at the Hilton Hawaiian Hotel from 10:00 am to 12:00 pm. Many people were still waiting in line when the ceremony was completed. I enjoyed signing autographs, and I was pleasantly surprised people wanted my autograph. After all, my war was over seventy years ago, and I wasn't famous, or a hero. But that didn't matter: the attendees were eager to meet us and hear our stories and to have us sign our names.

Signing Autographs at the Hilton Hawaiian Hotel. Jack is center right.

Next was a visit to the *Missouri* and the U.S.S. *Oklahoma* Memorial. The *Oklahoma* was sunk on December 7, 1941, and never recovered.

U.S.S. Oklahoma Memorial.

Next was the visit to the battleship U.S.S. *Utah* Memorial. This was a sunset ceremony honoring those lost aboard the ship on December 7, 1941. It so happened this ceremony included the sea burial of a *Utah* shipmate. His ashes were taken by two divers and placed inside the sunken *Utah*. He had had a long life and a good life after the war, but war is something that never leaves you. When he came to the end of his life, the decision was made to inter him with the men who had died on his ship, the men whose memories were never far from his mind even decades later.

U.S.S. Utah Memorial.

On Sunday the seventh, our first stop was the Pearl Harbor
Visitors Center. This was another long session of signing autographs
for a very responsive crowd. Later that day, we went to the *Oklahoma*
International commemoration. This memorial stands to honor the 429
sailors who lost their lives aboard the *Oklahoma* on December 7, 1941.
The memorial stands on the shores of Ford Island next to the former
berth of the *Oklahoma*. Those who escaped and swam ashore may have
walked or crawled across the ground we stood on that day, and to those
sailors it was a place of sanctuary, and for us a place to remember.

Pacific Aviation Museum.

For me, the highlight of the trip was the Pacific Aviation Museum
and the VP-23 squadron hangar where I had been posted seventy-three
years earlier. The building was untouched and had hundreds of bullet
holes from the Japanese attack on December 7, 1941. The VP-21
hangar, one hundred yards from ours, was where the first bomb fell on
Ford Island. It remains the same, heavily damaged. I walked down the
aircraft ramp to the edge of the water where I'd spent four months in
the beach crew. I then went to and spent time at the exact spot where

I'd spent three days and nights in the machine gun pit. Vivid memories ran rampant. I could still hear the ships and aircraft noise during blacked-out nights.

Sully Sullenberger and Jack Holder. This is the airline pilot who safely landed the Boeing 767 in the Hudson River.

Pearl Harbor International Parade

This was an occasion I will never forget. The twelve of us rode as Grand Marshals down the streets of Honolulu, each in a new Corvette convertible. The parade lasted one and a half hours and the crowd was estimated between eighty thousand to one hundred thousand people. It was a wonderful end to an amazing trip. Seven decades after the war, Americans still remembered and turned out in droves to thank us.

Everything, good or bad, has an end, and this journey was no different. I departed on December 8, 2014, from Honolulu back to Phoenix. My adventure was over, but it wasn't the last one I would have that involved commemorating the sacrifices of World War II veterans.

Ruth and Jack, Grand Marshall Parade, Phoenix, AZ, 2014.

December 7, 2014, Grand Marshal Parade down the streets of Honolulu.
Jack Holder and John Resig, president of Chive Industries.

In April 2015, I was treated by the Greatest Generation Foundation with a trip to Guam, Saipan, Tinian, and Iwo Jima. In commemoration of the 73rd anniversary of the battle for Iwo Jima, I spoke with so many gracious people in Guam and in Saipan of the atrocities they suffered at the hands of the Japanese during the war. I visited all the caves the Japanese had hidden their troops in and the remaining gun emplacements.

I walked down the Able 4 runway on the island of Tinian, the same runway used by Lieutenant Paul Tibbet to pilot the Enola Gay B-29 to Tokyo loaded with the atomic bomb. I stood on top Mt. Suribachi in Iwo Jima, overlooking the beach where we landed sixty thousand marines in 1945. Visiting these places reminded me powerfully of my own postings and experiences in the Pacific theater.

I have continued to travel and talk about my experiences in the war. In May of 2015, I was invited to Austin, Texas, by John Resig, president of the Chive Industries, for a live podcast. Governor of Texas Rick Perry joined us for this podcast. On May 12, 2015, I traveled to Huntington Beach, California, invited by Travis Brasher, the CEO of TravisMathew Apparel, for a presentation for their employees. On June 4, 2015, I was invited to Addison, Texas, and shared the stage with Governor Rick Perry when he announced his plans to run for president of the United States. On June 5, 2015, I gave a presentation on the Battle of Midway at the Arizona State Capital. On July 25, 2015, I was on the U.S.S. *Midway* in San Diego Harbor autographing books, and on August 12, 2015, I returned to the *Midway* for additional book signings.

Pearl Harbor: 74th Anniversary

ON DECEMBER SECOND OF 2015 I flew from Phoenix to Pearl Harbor for the 74th anniversary, where I met with the eleven other Pearl Harbor survivors. Again, we came from all over the country, from New Jersey to California. We made an early-morning trip the next day to Hickham Field Army Base to give a presentation to the local sixth-grade schoolchildren. I was first greeted by a schoolteacher, Cat Wailehua, who said to me, "Hey, I remember you, you were here last year!" Then, while we were having lunch with the children, a small girl sat down beside me and said, "I remember you gave a presentation to my class last year."

Later that day, we signed autographs at the Outrigger Hotel Resort. This went on for two and a half hours, and even when we stopped there were still many people standing in line.

I told one of the lady autograph-seekers that I was writing a book and hoped we could convince Clint Eastwood to make a movie out of it. She said, "You look like Clint Eastwood…or rather, Clint looks like you!" (I am sure she had poor eyesight.)

The following day, we visited Schofield Barracks Army Personnel to see their fleet of helicopters, and I had my picture taken in one of them. Later, we visited Wheeler Field to give another presentation to schoolchildren there. That night we had dinner at the Royal Hawaiian Hotel.

On December fifth we signed autographs again, at the Pearl Harbor Commemoration Center. Then we took a boat ride around Pearl Harbor and Ford Island, where my hangar was. Again, I couldn't believe what exhilaration it was, as we rounded the island, to view those old hangars I'd seen on that long-ago December seventh. All my memories of that day returned: Watching all those bombed and torpedoed ships down Battleship Row, sinking. Watching stranded seamen jumping ship and swimming through burning water. This was a devastation I will never forget. We then paid a visit to the U.S.S. *Arizona* Memorial.

The next morning at 6:00 am sharp we were at the battleship U.S.S. *Missouri* for a *FOX NFL Sunday* live broadcast with Terry Bradshaw, Jimmy Johnson, Howie Long and Michael Strahan. I had my picture taken with Bradshaw, and then, during an intermission when they brought out two marines to demonstrate pushups, I joined in. Later, when I asked Bradshaw how many we'd done, he said, "I don't know, but you lasted longer than they did!" Then he said, "I can't believe I just witnessed a ninety-four-year-old man doing pushups."

Jack joining marines for pushups, FOX NFL Sunday broadcast.

Terry Bradshaw and Jack Holder at FOX NFL Sunday broadcast.

The next day was the anniversary, and that night the twelve of us rode down the streets of Honolulu on the Corvettes in the Grand Marshal Parade. I rode along with a young ensign who was only three months out of the academy. The crowd was estimated to be over a hundred thousand that night.

Grand Marshal Parade, 2015. Esign Madison Cumbo, Jack Holder, and Lt. JG. Amber Loman.

I hope to continue to travel and speak at various events. I like being recognized for my service. When someone thanks me for serving, I know they are thanking all of us, especially the ones that didn't come home from the war. I especially like educating younger people about what we did and why.

World War II made America what it is today: a country full of people from many different places, but a country that pulls together when it's needful. When you go to work tomorrow, look around: chances are you'll see white people, black people, people whose parents speak Spanish, or Russian, or Chinese or Arabic. And as different as they might be from you, you all have something in common: you're all Americans.

The strength of this nation, I think, is this: on an average day, we're free to focus on our differences. But when we are threatened, it's as Americans that we respond to that threat. When that happens, where your people came from or what kind of food you make during the holidays or what church you worship at means little next to the fact that to be an American is to embrace those differences. What we have in common – being citizens of the "land of the free, and home of the brave" – is so much more important than how we differ.

When we are born, there is nothing written that we can see about how our lives are going to be directed and the experiences we are going to have. Each of us has our path. At a moment's notice, it can change. The question is, are we up to the task? I can answer that, because I lived through the greatest challenge to the American way of life we've ever faced. The answer is yes. We are up to the task. The ideas enshrined in the Constitution, and symbolized by the Statue of Liberty, are as important today as they ever were. We are from many lands, but we are all Americans. Together, we will face every challenge, and we will overcome them, because together we are strong.

Before my war, I was just another farm boy from Texas. After the war, I was still that farm boy, but I was something more: a true American. Not just because I served, but because I served with people from the many, many different versions of America. That taught me that "I'm a Texan" meant little compared to "I'm an American."

This nation has given me an amazing, adventurous and happy life. It's my belief that if you embrace what it means to be an American in its most grand sense, it will give you the same.